Poet, dramatist, and translator (*Mother Goose* and *Peanuts* into Japanese) Tanikawa Shuntaro has received the *Saida Takashi* Drama Prize, and the *Noma, Shogakkan, Hana-Tsubaki, Yomiuri* literary prizes, and (in translation by Elliott and Kawamura) the American Book Award.

He has read his work in Moscow, Leningrad, Berlin, Frankfurt, Zurich, Rotterdam, London, and, under the auspices of the Japan Society, the Academy of American Poets, the Library of Congress, and others, throughout the USA.

Tanikawa Shuntaro is contemporary Japan's most widely read poet ... and its most adventurous ....
                                                            Kitagawa Toru

Japanese names are given in the traditional order, family name first.

Diacritical signs unfamiliar to the general reader have been omitted. As a general rule in Japanese every letter is pronounced even when two identical letters appear in series in one word.

Asian Poetry in Translation: Japan
Editor, Thomas Fitzsimmons

#1 *Devil's Wind: A Thousand Steps* by Yoshimasu Gozo

#2 *Sun, Sand and Wind* by Shozu Ben

#3 *A String Around Autumn: Selected Poems 1952-1980*
      by Ooka Makoto

#4 *Treelike: The Poetry of Kinoshita Yuji*
      — Japan-US Friendship Commission Translation Prize

#5 *Dead Languages: Selected Poems 1946-1984* by Tamura Ryuichi

#6 *Celebration in Darkness: Selected Poems of Yoshioka Minoru*
      &
    Strangers' Sky: Selected Poems of Iijima Koichi

#7 *A Play of Mirrors: Eight Major Poets of Modern Japan*

#8 *A Thousand Steps ... and More: Selected Poems and Prose
      1964-1984* by Yoshimasu Gozo

#9 *Demented Flute: Selected Poems 1967-1986* by Sasaki Mikiro

#10 *I Am Alive: The Tanka Poems* of Goto Miyoko

#11 *Moonstone Woman: Selected Poems and Prose*
      by Tada Chimako

#12 *Self-Righting Lamp: Selected Poems* by Maruyama Kaoru

#13 *Mt. Fuji: Selected Poems 1943-1986* by Kusano Shinpei

#14 *62 Sonnets and Definitions* by Tanikawa Shuntaro

Supported by the National Endowment for the Arts, the Japan-US Friendship Commission, Oakland University (MI), University of Michigan Center for Japanese Studies, the Saison Cultural Foundation (Japan), the University of Sydney (Australia) and UNESCO.

62 Sonnets and *Definitions*
Poems and Prosepoems

Asian Poetry in Translation : Japan #14

Photograph by Momose Tsunehiko

62 Sonnets and *Definitions*

Poems and Prosepoems

Tanikawa Shuntaro

Translated by

William I. Elliott
Kawamura Kazuo

Introduction by Kitagawa Toru

Katydid Books   Santa Fe

Copyright © 1992 by Katydid Books
English translations Copyright © 1992 by William I. Elliott and Kawamura Kazuo
Preface and Afterword Copyright © 1992 by William I. Elliott
Introduction Copyright © 1992 by Kitagawa Toru
Photograph of Mr. Tanikawa Copyright © 1992 by Momose Tsunehiko
Cover art Copyright © 1992 by Karen Hargreaves-Fitzsimmons

Originally published as:

Rokujuni no sonetto, Tokyo Sogensha, 1953
Teigi, Shityosha, Tokyo, 1975

First Edition
All rights reserved

Produced by KT DID Productions

Printed in the United States of America
by Thomson-Shore, Dexter, MI

This book is printed on acid-free paper and its binding materials have been chosen for strength and durability.

KATYDID BOOKS:
K.H.-Fitzsimmons and T. Fitzsimmons, assisted by G.L. Robinson
#1 Balsa Rd., Santa Fe, New Mexico 87505-8736

Distributed by Univ. of Hawaii Press
2840 Kolowalu St, Honolulu, HI 96822
FAX: (808) 988-6052

Library of Congress Cataloging in Publication Data

Tanikawa, Shuntaro, 1931-
    [Rokujuni no sonetto. English]
    62 sonnets and definitions ; Poems and prosepoems / Tanikawa Shuntaro ; translated by William I. Elliott [and] Kawamura Kazuo. - - 1st ed.
        p.   cm. - - (Asian poetry in translation. Japan ; #14)
    Translations of: Rokujuni no sonetto and Teigi.
    ISBN 0-942668-35-9 (pbk.) : $14.95
    1. Tanikawa, Shuntaro, 1931-   - -Translations into English.
I. Elliott, William I. II. Kawamura, Kazuo, 1933-
III. Tanikawa, Shuntaro, 1931- Teigi. English. 1992. IV. Title : 62 sonnets and definitions. V. Title: Sixty-two sonnets and definitions. VI. Title: Poems and prosepoems. VII. Series.
PL862.A54A24   1992
895.6' 15- -dc20   92-4090
                                                                         CIP

Contents

Preface
by William I. Elliott 11

Introduction
by Kitagawa Toru 13

62 Sonnets 17

Definitions 81

Afterword
by William I. Elliott 115

Preface

William I. Elliott

As a teen-ager growing up in Tokyo, the only child of well-known philosopher and educator Tanikawa Tetsuzo, Shuntaro had already begun to write poetry. Just before graduating from high-school (in 1949) he announced that he did not wish to enroll in university. When his father asked what, then, did he wish to do, he had no clear answer. But he produced two notebooks of poems for his father's perusal. Professor Tanikawa, himself a good literary critic, read them and passed them in turn to well-known poet Miyoshi Tatsuji who promptly submitted some of them to *Bungakukai*, a leading commercial literary magazine. They were published and Tanikawa was paid. Even so, Tanikawa did not believe that he either could be or wanted to be a poet, yet he went on writing, trying to support himself in that way. It would be years before he would begin to feel that poetry was a viable career.

In 1952, at the age of twenty-one, his first volume, *Two Billion Light Years of Solitude*, hit the older generation of poets and the public, too, like a shot. A significant poet had come to light, and one who would go on producing significant poetry across the second-half of the present century. In 1992 Tanikawa turned sixty-one.

The common discovery that first successes are hard to follow did not hold true for Tanikawa. Not the kind of poet merely to go on repeating himself, he looked for and found other forms, other subjects; it is clear to see that now for four decades he has been the most tirelessly inventive poet in Japanese literary history. One consequence of his creative genius has been not one or two landmark volumes but indeed a handful of collections widely regarded as milestones in the history of modern Japanese poetry (which began shortly after the Meiji Restoration in 1868).

The presentation of *62 Sonnets* and *Definitions* brings together two of those books (written, respectively, in his twenties and forties). These poems are indeed light years removed from the traditional world of waka and haiku. In matters of length, subject matter and approach, for instance, the waka of the *Kokinshu* (992) and the haiku of Basho's *The Narrow Road to the Deep North* (begun in 1689) are very unlike the poems of *62 Sonnets* and *Definitions*. One thinks of the often quiet, wry, indirect approach to ideas and feelings that characterizes many classic poems; or of the proximity to nature that is maintained; or of the detatchment from worldly matters that underlies even a relishing of the beauty and pleasure the world affords. All of these elements, frequently found in waka and haiku, are sometimes at work in Tanikawa's poetry, have been from the earliest book and remain so today, yet he is a distinctly modern poet.

Neither Zen nor its presence in pre-modern Japanese poetry has had a direct influence on Tanikawa's work. He began with no knowledge of waka, haiku, Zen, or the modern Japanese poetic tradition. For that matter, he knew nothing about Western poetry. He began in all innocence, unencumbered with historical literary consciousness, and this may explain in part why his poetry is so free from convention. At the same time, he must have sat unconciously at his father's, and his culture's, feet, for his father had as one passion the arts associated with Zen, particularly those that pertain to gardens and the tea ceremony. Zen is many things to many people but it is true enough to state that in most Zen-related artistic practices one finds the elements of indirection, surprise, asymmetry, humor, engagement and detatchment, at least much of the time. Zen in this sense is discoverable in many waka and haiku, and also in Tanikawa's poetry, and this in spite of dissimilarties. One may remark it as perfectly predictably unpredictable that some elements of the Zen esthetic could be couched in semi-clinical, detached observations about a glass, toilet tissue or excreta as these are 'defined' in *Definitions*. And it may well be that his devotion to the ongoing translation of *Peanuts* traces to the Zen of Charlie Brown and associates as they go about quietly, wryly, humorously and briefly indentifying human glory and foibles. The funny bone of Issa the haiku poet would perhaps have responded delightedly to *Peanuts*.

Tanikawa is not, however, a Zen poet. That aside, he is the most 'popular' Japanese poet writing in the past half-century, who appeals to poet and non-poet alike in his finding ever new ways to regard the world from a stance that is in part recognizably traditional. He is very up-market in a basically traditonal way: a philosophically moderate, stylistically innovative man and poet. Parental blessing may be viewed as a blessing for him, for poetry, and for all readers. He is, like every major poet, inimitable.

Introduction

Kitagawa Toru

Tanikawa Shuntaro is contemporary Japan's most widely-read poet and one of its most adventurous with words. The two collections in this volume, *62 Sonnets* and *Definitions*, represent, respectively, these two features: his popularity, based on the wide sympathy of his readers, and his experiments in the frontiers of contemporary poetry. No other poet moves so freely between these two extremes.

It is not enough, however, to consider here only these two aspects, because the collections were written two decades apart and that fact makes a significant difference. *62 Sonnets* appeared in 1953, just a year after the appearance of *Two Billion Light Years of Solitude*, when he was twenty-two. *Definitions* on, the other hand came out twenty-two years later, in 1975, by which time he had published more than ten volumes of poetry. He was forty-four. Thus, while the sonnets might be called a product of his youth, *Definitions* abundantly represents his mature poetic power.

First of all, in terms of his personal poetic career, *62 Sonnets* is apt to be obscured by the first volume, *Two Billion Light Years of Solitude*, whose fresh cosmic intensity profoundly affected contemporary poetry. *62 Sonnets*, however, has a freshness comparable to that of the preceding volume. Mainstream Japanese poetry at that time was a "poetry that thinks' and therefore a poetry, as it were, that is self-denying and was largely conceptual in the existential sense. *62 Sonnets* appeared in this context as a poetic language that boldly affirmed the priviledged sensitivity of the younger generation and at the same time avoided the oppressive language of ideas. The collection sings of the joy of *carpe diem*, of sunny solitude, and of the fertility of life, and all this without affectation. In his essay 'About My Work' Tanikawa states 'As a whole *62 Sonnets* is, if I may exaggerate, a song in praise of life. At the time I was at a peak of physical exuberance and I was unashamedly sensitive to the whole experience.'

We should note, however, that his 'I', though thus affirmed, is not personal assertion at all. The 'I' tries to grow transparent and melt into nature like wind, light and clouds, and seeks to become its own mysterious universe. The ubiquitous essence of this amorphous 'I' seems to have required the intense lyricism of the sonnet form.

By contrast, *Definitions* can be regarded as the opposite poetic methodology, because while *62 Sonnets* stands as 'a song in praise of life,' *Definitions* tries radically to suppress the lyrical bent. The poet's attitude is rather prosaic in that he wishes to describe 'things' with maximum exactitude.

This attempt is clearly suggested by the fact that 'Citation Concerning the Meter Standard' is placed at the book's very beginning. Consisting of a faithful quotation from an encyclopedia, this piece is itself a model of exact definition. It is written in the language of scientific reasoning, poles apart from that of poetry. But here the poet is parodying the generally accepted notion of 'definition', according to which there is only one definition, scientifically speaking, by which to describe a thing. Under the disguise of the prosaic formality of 'definition' as used in scientific writings or in civic laws, the poems aim, we might say, to stretch the area of the arbitrariness and the pluralism inherent in 'definition.' The more exactly the poet tries to write about familiar things—call it our world—it is not 'things' themselves but the operation of words and imagination in reaching those 'things' that matters most.

Take, for example, a poem called 'Impossible Approach to a Glass'. A glass is, in terms of its practical use, nothing more than 'an instrument whose chief purpose is the satisfaction of our thirst.' But once the poet departs from its defined utility and begins to try to describe a glass as it is, there appears an object which will be associatively or imaginatively described according to shape, space, mass and sound, and in the possibility of its broken pieces being used as weapons. In order to approach 'things' the poet's experience of words and imagination has to be engaged. When the poet sets out aiming not to arrive at 'things' but to reach them through words and imagination, *Definitions* suddenly turns into poetry.

I have perhaps over-distinguished the difference between these two collections. Contrary as their methods may be, however, the two have in common that they try to grasp the world as unknown and mysterious. No, grasping is not all the poems do. In that the 'I' of *62 Sonnets* is not self-assertive but has become a free floating movement of words, the world emerges in its mysteriousness. There is, in my judgement, a coherence in Tanikawa's poems no matter how varied his methods.

62 Sonnets

Shadows of Trees

And yet there is joy in this day
as in the heart of the young sun.
Of this joy the world of tables, guns and gods
is altogether unaware.

Only to this place
where people are standing
do shadows of trees lead their hearts home,
enveloped in this day's humility.

When I read the sky, sing of clouds,
or murmur in joy,
as in prayer,

Sun and trees alike look upon
both what I've forgotten
and what I endlessly recall.

Longings

Under the shadow of early summer sun's destiny,
my hopes neglected,
my longings race around
before I remember the transience of things.

Knowing that fields and clouds are merely foolish,
how could we think that someone was enticing us
with all the lovely forms which I have loved
(without believing in them)?

Around my small grave, before long,
man, rock, and sky will remain.
But who can go on recalling tomorrow?

I've forgotten even God. Under the sway
of early summer sun's young destiny,
if you didn't live at all how could anything happen?

Homecoming

This was an alien land.
I was drawn by the deep darkness of a side door
of this wretched earth;
drawn by the utterly eerie look of the rooms.

Who am I?
I don't know how to go back home.
I keep on writing letters
about my finite sojourn here.

No other planet attracts me.
This one will do—even better than eternity;
but, 'P.S. Someday I may try to go home.'

I will be going home some day
from this familiar alien land.
A homecoming I don't know about when I am no more.

Today

Sunday again
and Monday's cloudy again
and then turns sunny;
and who knows what's next?

Next? I have no idea.
There's only today. There's no 'again' in me—
only 'today.'

I remember nothing but today.
Death would be 'today'
and living is intensely 'today.'

I love today
until a short song dies
and today is devoted to brief mourning.

Incidental Thoughts

So this is life after all?
People swarm the sun-swept morning streets;
children pass by, laughing like sparrows;
illusions whirl along like wind.

Today sings before eternity,
its song both younger
and more abstruse.
It sings more eternally than eternity.

In cities and villages, on deserts and seas,
talking goes on and on—amusing, awful and sad;
empty arguments rage and eyes burn day in and out.

So this is life after all?
Today this star is filled with so many tantalizing things
that God is nearly forgotten.

Morning (1)

Skies are so overcast
that this passing night is hidden.
Young hope whispers,
'So today has begun again.'

I have no time or place to start from.
I just live,
killing my days,
my heart alone overflowing.

I trust this full heart;
trust its meaningless tears,
though I lack both serenity and assurance.

Morning is cloudy.
In the ubiquitous silence, night still lingering,
my heart, my poor puny heart, overflows.

Morning (2)

I was singing a morning meal,
painting the heart's liquid refreshment.
Are this-and-that linked
in this portent of a vast harmony?

Dressed in white, I woke up at light's delight
and the pangs of awakening
to feel and sing anew,
my heart no longer sleeping.

Death comes out of the earth,
out of the future.
People die today and are left in ignorance.

But the heart must go on, responsive to everything,
always starting to live anew, beginning here
and negotiating the distances.

Laughing

I'm neither unhappy enough
to forget unhappiness
nor happy enough
to forget happiness.

The sun keeps speaking of day,
and the stars of night;
or say, rather, that a most beautiful silence
speaks of my heart and mine alone.

What is does not flow.
What comes and goes knows
nothing but this present moment.

To question the present moment is forbidden;
and one day, before this moment ends,
people may break out laughing.

Bewilderment

Society is nothing but
a human logjam;
and loneliness nothing but
one miserable specimen.

Bewilderment.
I'm completely bewildered.
God uses me
and politicians try to, too.

All kinds of things—girls, catching a cold, philosophy—
all these bewilder me.
Fate wants to work in detail.

And so this line of verse as a diversion.
No one cares what I say:
Will that make some fool think I'm a loner?

The Unknown

Bicycle said,
'Pencil' and chemistry said,
'Man, you made me.'

What did the badger think?
A star?
What did *God* think
of the foolish arrogance of this excessive passion?

Then let them die haphazardly one by one,
those who have forgotten what loneliness is:
'Here vanish the unknown.'

Wind blew over the earth and an unknown star.
God walked on the earth at evening,
and also on an unknown star.

Silence

Even when silence had given a name to everything
that my heart had welcomed,
suddenly I was frightened,
overcome by the awe of being unknown.

What words remain after the voice is lost?
What sort of heart beyond sadness?
And what sort of health is there between living and dying?
I started to whisper 'God,' but didn't.

It is always I who am responsible to talk
about myself, about the world,
knowing that I know nothing.

Not a word, not a voice,
no murmur, no song—not even a cough, yet
I have to talk about everything.

Ruins

No prayers of petition,
no philosophy to curse Him with;
if anything, there was only just
a faint song of God himself, next to nothingness.

I shall never sing again
of yesterday's undoubted happiness,
of tomorrow with its promise of sorrow,
nor of today, skies clear to the point of vanity.

Ruins are the bones of time.
Just as today's wind blows towards oblivion,
the meaning of man vanishes into an utterly clear sky.

Ruins aspire only to keep standing
under the young sun. Nothing else.
They hope only to keep standing.

Now

Brilliance can illuminate anything.
As long as I live in the present moment
and love it unstintingly,
everything kindly forgets me.

In a song that is ever silent
signs of God are faintly felt
and all at once, in this silent sweep of space,
I am conscious of this moment.

When I believe in this moment in all its richness,
even though I am aware of death,
I am free.

Passion can fill anything
under the silently shining sun and sky,
which are overflowing.

In the Field

My heart removed me to a height
from which I looked down on time.
I was recollected
and God's capriciousness glimpsed.

Without a song, without will,
I'm just like a grade school boy eager to go home.
On such a fine day as this
who could possibly atone for what?

People sing amiss.
They have no words to utter nothingness
and no words to utter anything.

But where I'm standing there is everything:
people on the street, grass in the field, and,
in the heavens, nothingness.

Mold

Clouds were roughly cast.
Distant mountains were trying to endure sunlight.
The landscape darkened over and cast shadows
that resembled the rough mold of my heart.

The landscape is the mold of my joy,
a negative space waiting for joy;
but the landscape must be filled
and can never become joy itself.

It's not sorrow that molds joy.
In the unknown, unfinished capriciousness of things
my heart received no name.

But once fulfilled and molded,
the darkening landscape and my unnamed heart
will be completely forgotten.

Morning (3)

The lamp was on all night.
A letter came at dawn.
The sky is lazy,
the children still asleep.

I get up,
throw some things away,
pick up, and get busy.

People start walking,
I begin to forget,
and God starts weeping.

I am suddenly aware that at nightfall everything will vanish.
And just at that moment
first light breaks.

Beginning

When I'm alone
I fall into a reverie
where time overtakes me.
Smiling wryly,

I escape;
but come too close again.
Touching the forms of terrible things
makes me conscious of a single heart.

Feigning ignorance,
I package time and send it
in the direction of yesterday.

Yet some things I can't get rid of.
I cling to those and find suddenly
a new beginning.

Mirror

As I listen to the sounds of my heart
my own contours grow hazy.
The heart, remembered,
grows feeble unless it moves.

Whatever is is outside of me,
and when I try to enter
I am refused.
My heart wearies.

Inside of me there's only a thinking mirror,
which, too docile,
reflects everything it sees.

Things reflected are no longer existing things.
In an effort to get out, I look at the mirror.
My inner reflected form recedes but never vanishes.

Expansion

I keep on walking
through the expansion of things.
At the wind's sudden rising
time stirs.

But subtle gestures
are soon forgotten.
In the expansion of which no one is aware,
time dies.

Let's always be aware of an expansion beyond imagining.
Let's learn to live and die
surrounded by indifferent things.

I keep on walking as if I, too, were a thing.
I stop looking and all at once
I begin to live.

Concerning my Heart

Gradually I grow familiar with living.
Having believed till now only in forms,
I've known nothing of the heart
and that made my solitude all the more cheerful.

Maybe I was tired of my heart.
Every resolute form
lives its time and occupies space
more assuredly than my heart.

I have no song now.
I have a common origin with stars.
Whatever begot me had no heart.

Aware of that, my heart suddenly returns.
Is that because my form is ugly?
No. Because the world is too beautiful.

Song

When I looked up
those clouds were gone.
Not in the amorphous clouds but outside them,
there's a feeling I'm familiar with.

Ancient prayers continuously rain down curses
on those forms.
When heaven is vacant and earth holds a heart,
clouds, suspended, aspire to be more than they are.

But what could they become?
Softly, as though they hope to have hearts,
they go on annihilating their own shapes.

A full earth
and a vacant sky
move me to song.

Concerning Forms

Forms foreboding and vanished
fill the excessively clear sky,
the forms themselves invisible,
like the human heart.

Real forms have no hearts.
Forms are transient.
It is forms that fear both
ugliness and destruction.

And yet our joy is in trusting in
and loving forms;
or rather in trusting in a heart beyond forms.

Today under this too clear sky
there is only one heart
and round about us only forms are beautiful.

Clouds

Clouds were really beautiful this morning.
Though lacking hearts, they seemed illumined by one heart.
They were like a brief consolation;
they accepted their own luminosity and then floated away ....

I can believe in lots of things
and love them.
It's they that keep me going;
give me heart.

Her heart in its transiency
is hard to measure,
being too far or too near ....

But, assured of their time and place,
trees live, and she lives.
This morning the letter I wrote was not addressed to the heart.

Dreams

For a moment, as if everything were a radiant lie,
I was awake in my dreams. No proof remains, except
I remember being happy.

In her absence
I trust too much in everything.
When I let in unhappiness
suddenly a slight anguish assails me.

A tree's shape ... the sea's ... the sun's ....
I think of her in that setting,
her shape itself like the soul's.

I used to be too wide-awake.
I'll sleep undisturbed today
to prove the weight of my dreams.

25

In the midst of the world, I stir;
so does the world, faintly.
As the world casually looks back
celestial birds are startled and fly away.

The sky is suddenly empty.
Written words are blinding.
I shade my eyes and see
nothing but distant mountains.

Time grows tired.
I don't know how to take care of him.
The sky puffs itself up.

I keep on walking.
The world is watching me.
I turn my eyes away, towards death.

26

She walks towards me.
We pass each other; I love her.
But distance outdistances us
and oblivion overtakes her.

When I go shopping in the city
they give me my change in solitude.
I walk around aimlessly,
thinking how to use that change.

Of a sudden a flag signs the air.
The particles of time I throw at it
shatter twilight.

I start to go back but forget how I should walk.
Night begins to lure me
but certain signs suggest tomorrow will be hard on me.

27

Earth is heavy with a child of fire.
Since no birth is forthcoming
clouds wish to be dabs of cotton for death.
But clouds weep too much.

The clock keeps complaining to time.
When time gets bored
even cats yawn.
I grow as lonely as an island.

By day, night is accused;
by night, day is accused.
I want to defend both.

I casually stand up
and the world follows me.
I go into a restroom.

28

When I try to sleep
dreams get in my eyes.
Pain wakens me.
I measure philosophy's transparency.

Flowers carry on their own lives.
I touch a lot of lives as I stroll along.
My fingers gradually grow numb
and are finally frostbitten by death.

I dance
and knock everything down.
The world becomes a toy horn.

I am tired
and now I can sleep,
but can't forget how black the dreamless night.

29

I'm copying down my memories.
Old visions are all good ones.
The winter sunlight that warms my fingers
also falls across today's empty chair.

Between the window's outside and inside
a fragment of the world is suspended.
As I reach to touch it
the beautiful thing gallops away.

I keep gazing at everything.
My heart reluctantly whispers
but love hushes it.

Today returns;
yesterday is a blur;
I can't imagine the shape of tomorrow.

30

I won't let words rest.
At times they feel ashamed of themselves
and want to die, inside of me.
When that happens I'm in love.

In a world otherwise silent
people—only people—chatter away.
What's more, sun and trees and clouds
are unconscious of their beauty.

A fast-flying plane flies in the shape of a human passion.
Though the blue sky pretends to be a backdrop,
in fact there's nothing there.

When I call out, in a small voice,
the world doesn't answer.
My words are no different from those of the birds.

31

Sitting down in the world in a chair prepared for me,
I suddenly cease to be.
I shout.
Only words survive.

God has smeared false pigments across the heavens.
When we try to imitate those hues,
pictures die; and we die.
Trees alone stand strong against the heavens.

I bear witness in the midst of a festival.
I keep on singing
and happiness comes to measure my height.

I read a book of time.
Everything is recorded there—and therefore nothing.
I bombard yesterday with questions.

32

Sometimes time dances
and I snatch fragments of eternity,
measuring my life's length
and anticipating things to come.

The wind rises.
I plan a future based on memories.
The sun is high. To live summer over again—my resolution!

So mixed regrets and forebodings
have built up inside of me.
As those age I shall grow intimate with death.

But today I'm still annoyed by growing pains.
It's like the labor that promises birth.
I start running; I have a life to waste.

33

I tried getting closer
but backed off again;
tried backing off
but again drew near.

Always in utter self-forgetfulness
my mind gestures fantastically.
In trying to find the mind's order
I get lost in the human woods.

My excuse is always the joy of life.
My love is leaping
and is at times indifferent to everything.

The blue sky is not a roof but an old well.
I throw myself in,
only to be reborn.

34

Thanks to wind, trees know the joy of movement.
The sun, posing as a midwife,
looks conceited and young for its age.
I smell the sun.

The music ends.
Life's moment fills me.
My head droops
and happiness takes notice.

Since I've nothing to do with life
I just keep singing.
But I know how to praise.

When I at last reach the blue of the sky
there'll surely be no one there.
That sky is a benevolent lie.

35

When I return from town
silence nonchalantly occupies the room.
I open the window without a word
and a black picture flows in.

Under the streetlight's gaze
night's mutterings grow conspicuous,
Inside me are pictures of the seasons.
Unlived in, they are extravagantly beautiful.

Voices come from far away,
calling no one
but merely tossed up to the sky.

My daytime pupils aren't stretched open yet.
Things in the dark are hard to distinguish;
stars alone abound.

36

I've looked too long at the light—
my shadow is pitch black.
I try to calculate my loneliness
but there's no solution.

All distances return to me again.
Intimate with no one save myself,
I've no place to dispose of my words.
I plot to convert them into sweat.

The heavens are forever a tedious stage setting.
Since everything is under them,
they become the measuring rod of distance.

Yet when I try to don sentimentality,
unfortunately I find the sleeves too short.
I recall my infancy.

37

I go back into myself.
No one's there.
Where do I come from?
I was born of infinity.

I'd like to be everywhere at once, like light.
What an insolent wish that is!
Song-like, my love is always thrown away,
unable to become even a mild breeze.

We go on living
and finally grow aware of love.
And there's no place to send it. Like nostalgia.

People have to use up love,
say, in songs or sweat;
or change it into other forms.

38

Since I came to life
the story can't end.
If we can't ever forget things
then old gods can't sleep.

There's a midnight exchange
of tiny whispered words.
The songs of day are frozen
and over them whispers keep on sliding.

The shapes of life are sharpened
in the silence
after the shrill cry of sinister birds.

I'm the story-teller.
After the wind has borne my ineloquence away
from the distance 'Love ...' comes back.

39

Clouds fill up and dispose of themselves:
why is that rain?
People dispose of their overflowing hearts:
why is that a song?

The faint-hearted go on
calling the things in the world;
yet trees don't reply—
they're too busy becoming the world.

When people realize they are part of an extension
they start talking tough; e.g.,
'I'm more important than trees.'

Thus, inaudibly, the trees whisper,
'It's important not to sing
but to empty your hearts.'

40

When I dream of where the distances end,
things at hand begin to murmur.
Because love is a drifter
it always comes back perspiring.

Even running off to some forsaken place
and coming back hungry,
it has no happy place to call its own.
Night, as usual, is cold to lonely love.

As though in a changing of absences,
there's night and then there's day.
And love cannot seek shelter there.

When I'm gone
the night that lingers is lovely,
and seems oblivious of me.

41

Gazing at the blueness of the sky
makes me feel I've a place to go back to,
though the escaped brightness has none.

Sunlight everlastingly lavishly expends itself.
Even after dark, people are busy picking up its pieces.
We are basely born
and don't know how to rest well, like the trees.

The window contains what is overflowing.
I am estranged from people
because I want no room except the universe.

To be is to injure space and time,
and the pain reproaches me.
When I'm gone my health will return.

42

Seen through sunlight, the sky ...
and the color of nothing is beautiful.
To time's gentle questioning
I do not reply.

Bring back yesterday morning!
For the vanished scenery
all I can do is
mourn.

Today, expectation looks like tomorrow.
Tomorrow, expectation is
merely today.

A fine day surrounds me.
Since my childhood, what kinds of things have I liked?
Nearby, there are signs of rebirth.

43

Clouds collect
the sky's overflowing light.
Wind whispers in my ear
and suddenly a great emptiness awakens.

Turning, I see someone.
I quietly leave my words behind.
People treat them politely.
I sit on the world, as on a chair.

People collect
the sounds of the earth.
But no secret murmurings will persuade me.

Yet sometimes a wind-like happiness emerges
from among things indifferent to me,
and when it does I am here again.

44

Because I'm a fighter
the blue sky is my shield
and I prowl the night.
I've aimed at something beyond the world, but ....

While my empty eyes roam around
I go on fighting, though there's no foe.
When the world coughs in the darkness
I brace myself and stand ready.

Unknown things inside and out,
and how those are connected,
dazzle me.

My blood ebbs away.
I feel bound by dim memories
and am no longer brave.

45

In a fierce wind
the earth is like a kite.
Even at high noon
we are aware of night.

Wordless, the fretful wind
can only run around.
I think of the wind on another star—
Can they be friends?

We have night and day on earth.
Meantime, what are other stars doing?
How do they endure expanding in silence?

Blue sky lies.
While we sleep night whispers the truth.
Then in the morning we say we dreamed.

46

The young sun briefly illumines
my inner world that opens on the night.
Particles of dust are swarming in the sun.
Do they foretell illness?

When did my feet steal from the ground,
like the roots of a great flourishing tree?
When did I embrace the sky before praising the daytime,
like young branches?

It's silly trying to understand night.
The best I can do is leave sleeping things alone,
even if I must stop singing gentle lullabies.

Everything should be silent at night,
asking nothing of the stars,
because they won't even smile coldly.

47

Time saturates the cloudy night sky;
falls like snowflakes, when I stir.
My heart feels cold;
only my blood is warm.

Things enjoyable by day hold their breath—
when I chase them they're no longer there.
Imaginary months and years fill my head.
I set them afire.

Memories burn;
premonitions burn;
today is left a heap of ashen embers.

I can't really believe my own existence
and so I am given tomorrow in exchange for my dreams.
When I awaken, breakfast is in the air.

48

We often hear the dark side of life
referred to solemnly:
graves, hearses, wills ....
These tell us nothing about death.

The living cannot see beyond shadows
and don't know what it's like to lose nothing.
Surrounded by mirrors,
we're always peeping into life in reflection.

Since death lacks mirrors
we shall soon be unselfconscious
and able to be one with the world ....

But in the rainy street today the living are busy living.
The evening paper reports suicides:
we're nothing but the distance that surrounds death.

49

Who could know of my death
in the midst of love?
Let me nurture desire in all its tenderness
so as to snatch love back from the world.

I look at her
and life's shapes bring me back to the world.
A young tree and her figure
sometimes meet in me.

What I learn in touching her closed lips,
without naming my feelings,
is carried away by a vast silence.

Yet in that moment I am also that silence.
Like a tree, I, too,
snatch love from the world.

50

At times the stillness of existence
is fainter than the stillness of nothingness.
Yet let us draw near
and the subtle stirrings of stillness are revealed.

Don't things complain in their anxiety
about just being called
a cup, a tree,
a daughter, a picture ...?

I know that things certainly do exist,
but can you name anything
apart from people?

It's fairly easy for nothing to exist.
Call as I will, the world doesn't waken.
All I can do is love foolishly.

51

Even being here in this familiar scenery
I find the world's complexity bewildering.
I'd rather know things here and now
than things and places distant.

The single-mindedness of things foredoomed tempts me
towards simple thoughts;
only, in this familiar moment
death will not inhibit my thoughts.

Under the silence of sky and sun
this moment is constantly being snatched away,
and the pain of it scares me.

But I return into the world.
No day is without its partings, is it?
To that world I return.

52

As I stroll along this field,
the kind and cunning sky hiding nothingness
behind its back,
I wonder what kind of wind blows in that forest?

Every time I prepare to go home
something invariably escapes me.
I feel surrounded by things not myself,
and in order to sustain them grow tired.

But briefly the sun indiscretely illumines everything
and in that stark naked scenery
my shadow is blacker than night.

And my absence is filled with trees, clouds and people.
My love bears them witness
and I begin to depend on my absence.

53

A cloudy day. No shadows.
And I watched my words sicken.
Trees and grasses sang my songs;
my longings always came back down to earth.

Following the first ominous silence
we plunged pell-mell into a world of loquacity.
If words find their answers among people
they always fall ill apart from people.

I wish my words were as whole as the trees and grass
in that first silence
out of which everything was born.

What words know me intimately?
Instead of myself singing
I'd like hearing myself being sung.

54

I grew unwittingly apart
from the world in which I was born
and can no longer walk again
among the things of the earth.

We know that even love is a possession,
but we can't keep from praying
that life will go on.
And we accept the poverty of our prayers.

I can possess nothing,
though I love
trees, clouds, people.

I can only discard
my overflowing heart—
hesitant to call that an act of love.

55

Even just sitting around
I make my life bear fruit,
not unlike trees that, immobile,
move in the cosmic circle of life.

That I may play sincerely
all the days allotted me
I just keep standing,
until I wither.

I am a discarded vessel
in the shape of waiting,
knowing I'll never be filled.

If I have in this world a part to play,
it is that:
just standing.

56

Isn't the world a puny star in the middle of nowhere?
Twilight ...
the world stands by idly,
as if ashamed of itself.

In such moments
I collect the little names of things
and somehow
I lapse into silence.

Now and then sounds call to the world,
more confidently than my song:
 distant whistles, barking, the paper-boy ...

In such moments the world is listening,
as breathlessly as twilight,
reaffirming itself sound by sound.

57

In the song I sing
the world is wounded.
I try to make it sing
but it stays silent.

Words are poor little kids
forever lost,
who perch on things, like dragonflies trembling
in the midst of dense silence.

They try to escape into things;
but words cannot
love the world.

They curse me and die,
snatched up by a star-bright sky.
I sell their corpses.

58

It's distance that makes
mountains mountains.
Looked at closely,
they start to resemble me.

Vast panoramas stop people in their tracks
and make them conscious of the engulfing distances.
Those very distances make people
the people they are.

Yet people also contain distances
inside themselves,
which is why they go on yearning ....

They soon find they're just places violated by distances,
and no longer observed.
They have become scenery.

59

Speaking worn-out words,
or rather no words,
and only having a heart capable of feeling,
I was content.

Falling rain ...
a girl running ...
and oh—the wind:
these are already my song.

Over and over, tirelessly,
I call the world's names—
the names of things I love.

And at times
as I persist in praising even unhappiness,
I become its godfather.

60

Just as wind rustles leaves
the world ruffles my mind.
Though I speak of sadness and joy,
my heart remains unnamable.

The world moves endlessly, expanding,
and I can never catch up.
I continue searching for my heart
in twilight or in rain or in cirrus clouds.

I am sometimes equal to the world's demands.
I yield myself
to sunlight, wind, the seasons—

—I become the world
and if for love's sake I no longer sing
I have no regrets about it.

61

The mind softly touches the world
and continues nodding in the shape of the world.
The wind rises ...
a boy is running ....

The mind also touches itself;
in order to sing, even tentatively,
it returns to itself,
one with the world.

Who will catch my songs of praise?
It's better for joy to return to earth,
for then joy doesn't die in solitude.

You don't need to confess
love.
The world will see it in your eyes.

62

Because the world loves me—
now tenderly,
now harshly—
I can bear any length of solitude.

When I was first given someone to love
I listened to nothing but the world's sounds.
Only simple sorrow and joy are clear to me,
for I always belong to the world.

I throw myself into
sky, trees, people,
that I may soon become part of the world's richness.

. . . I call to her.
The world turns to me
and I vanish.

Definitions

Citation Concerning the Meter Standard

The meter standard is a platinum bar alloyed with 10% of iridium. It is 102cm long and has an X-shaped cross section called the 'tresca section.' Across each of the polished oval surfaces near the bar's ends, three fine parallel lines are engraved. The meter *per se* was defined as the distance between each of the middle lines when the Standard was symmetrically supported by two rollers of at least 1cm in diameter placed parallel to each other at a distance of 572mm under standard atmospheric pressure and at 0° centigrade. (The standard bar, made in 1888 of ground metal, is now kept in the International Metric Office in the suburbs of Paris.) The Japanese Meter Standard, which is No.22, was made at the same time as the international bar and its length was 1m - 0.78, according to the periodic checkings conducted during 1920-22. Japan, however, amended the measurement method in 1961 and now defines length by light waves, so that the Meter Standard is no longer used.

from *Heibonsha's Encyclopedia*

A Very Difficult Thing

Its surface is gray and white, its volume evidently less than half a cubic meter. 'Soft White Scottie R Free Fold' is printed on the sides. There are exactly 400 sheets of soft white paper, their uses left to the buyer. I just now tore off the first sheet and blew my nose.

   Since it does occupy a certain amount of space, it is naturally subject to the mode of existence called time. I cannot say with any assurance whether it is beautiful or ugly. Do you really need additional clues?

A Statement about Not Telling This Thing's Name

Its upper edges, shaped like the teeth of a saw, must have been cut by some sharp tool. The lower edges are bent away so that I can't see them, but it is most likely that lower and upper edges have the same shape; and left and right edges are cut at right angles to upper and lower edges. By thus describing it I have clarified the shape of this thing in terms other than those of size and texture.

With a ruler I could easily specify its size, but since units such as centimeters and inches are relative I would really rather be more exact by saying that I guess the two longer sides (along upper and lower edges) are about 1.2 times longer than my index finger while the two shorter sides are shorter than that.

Although I could describe it more precisely if I picked it up and measured it, for some reason it seems to me untouchable. Because I wish to attribute a modest amount of sanctity to the act of linguistic description, I feel that I should hold to a certain asceticism.

Now, the limited sense of sight tells me that it is a shining, extremely thin silver substance. From past experience we must judge it to be apparently some sort of paper. Its surface is not smooth but looks like pear-skin on which many groups of letters reading "HARIS" are stamped as a design.

I of course know perfectly well this thing's specific name. It is not to pretend ignorance that I fail to divulge it here. It's merely that this is the very subject of this essay. And neither will I explain why and how this thing has come to be lying accidentally (and therefore already by necessity) before me. For to do so would naturally demand of me both a different subject and a different method from those employed here.

Morning Song Sung by a Clown

I suspect that it exists; that it really *is* something.

No one has ever stated its contours but I think they *are* clear. I don't think it'll stay in the same position forever, but *right now I* think it's reflecting a little light, even casting a shadow. It can't *not be,* and somehow it *is* like something.

But if it's something, it cannot, I *think,* be thought unimportant even if no one uses it. For some reason I feel as though I *want it to be* something. I wonder whether it's impossible for it not to be something. If it's not something, what in the world can it be? It can be that there isn't anything except something, *can't it?*

Since it's not at all indistinct, it's something after all, *isn't it?* If it's something, don't we think that it *should be* something about which we can't ask what it is? Something which we can' t answer is nothing? Some something which is not *some* thing?

Because it's too easy, for instance, to say shellfish or rope or dizziness, I pray that it be something to the degree that it's nothing other than something. Just lying there or floating.

(I honestly wish the world would begin there—I don't think I'd mind if it ended.)

The Dignity of Something which is Nothing

Something which is nothing is lying there just like something which is nothing and there's a relationship of nothing between these two somethings that are nothing. I don't know how to ask why something as nothing came to exist in this world. This something as nothing can always be found lying about everywhere and doesn't, for the time being, threaten our existence, but we are forever disturbed because of the very nothingness of this something which is nothing.

Sometimes this something as nothing touches our hands with its thick hair and sometimes is quite visually appealing on account of its dazzling sheen. We are sometimes deafened by its din and sometimes our tongues are stimulated by its tartness. But when compared with another something which is nothing, this something as nothing utterly loses its quality of nothingness. To understand this something as nothing as a boundless wholeness does not preclude understanding it in its multiple minute parts, but some- (The words following have been erased.)

—The present writer cannot describe something which is nothing as something as nothing. He always finds himself talking about something which is nothing as something which is something. To measure its size, discuss its utility and/or inutility, claim it's existence or describe the feel of the texture only serves to add to the illusion about this something which is nothing. It's up to the reader to judge whether my inability to define this something which is nothing is a result of the structure of language or of the style of writing or a defect of my intelligence.

Scissors

This thing lying on the desk is now being seen by my eyes. I could pick it up at this moment. I could cut out a human figure with it. I might even cut off all my hair. Though it's understood that murder is out of question.

Yet this thing also keeps getting rustier, blunter and older. It's still useful but it'll be thrown away before long. Although I have no way of knowing whether it's made of ore from Chile or whether Krupp's fingers have touched it, it's not hard to imagine that it will finally return to its indeterminate destiny, moving away from its human formality back to its original state. This thing here on the desk is at this moment talking about such a time, not to anyone in particular but coldly, silently, as if it were not doing that. People manufactured this for practical purposes and yet it has inevitably come to exist here in this way before and apart from any practical purpose it might later have. It's something which could be variously named—not just 'scissors.' It already has countless other names. Habit alone keeps me from using the other names. Or is it out of self-defense?

Because this thing, existing like this, has the power to extract words from me so that I go on being unreeled in this string of words and am always on the dangerous verge of being reduced to a far thinner and feebler existence than that of the scissors.

Impossible Approach to a Glass

In most cases it has a bottom but no top and is cylindrical. It is a cavity standing upright, an enclosed space closed towards the center of gravity. It can contain a given amount of liquid, without permitting it to spread, within the field of gravity. When it contains only air, we say it is empty, but even then its outline is clearly revealed by light, and the existence of its mass can be ascertained, without instrumentation, at a clear-headed glance.

When we flick our nails against it it vibrates and produces sound. It is sometimes used as a signal, and rarely as a unit of music. Its sound has a sort of stubborn self-sufficiency with no outside application and it threatens our ears. It is set on a table. Over and over again a hand grasps it. Often it slips from our hands. We can indeed deliberately fragment it, easily, and so it contains potential as a weapon. Even shattered, however, it still exists. If at this very moment all the glasses on earth were suddenly broken, we could still not escape its existence. Though its name varies from one culture to another because of various systems of transcription, it already exists for us as one common fixed idea, and even if its actual manufacture (from glass, wood, iron, clay) were to be forbidden under pain of death, we should nonetheless still be unable to escape the nightmare of its existence.

It is an instrument whose chief purpose is the satisfaction of our thirst, and under extreme circumstances it has no more use than a hollow formed by two cupped palms, but in the context of multiple forms of contemporary life it doubtless maintains silence as a form of beauty, now in the morning sunlight, now under artificial light.

Our intelligence, our experience and our skill have produced it on this earth and named it, and we refer to it by a single series of sounds as though it were completely natural, but as to what it truly is no one can claim to have an exact answer.

On the Pain and Pleasure of Looking at a Glass

On a wooden table stands a transparent glass which contains water. Right now a 60 watt bulb on the left, shining obliquely from above, throws a prism of light on a portion of the glass cylinder, but that in no way modifies the glass and the water. The contained water is not meant to slake thirst, but it seems that some family member (probably a child) may have put it there for no reason at all or, therefore, as it were, just for fun, and although it is a highly commonplace sight it compels a kind of tension in anyone who looks at it. This tension, it would seem, arises neither from the fragility that the feel of the glass suggests nor from the possibility of its being transformed suggested by the feel of the water, but, to the contrary, from the sense of their immobility. Although the cup and the water (and the soft shadow they cast on the table) could be destroyed in an instant by anyone's extended hand, the fact of their prior existence could not be denied.

Their immobility, even though having no relation to eternity, yet looms as a riddle to all men; therefore, there can be no language in which to describe or explain them, and no painting or sculpture, either, with which to picture or mold them. This fact however, does not make them any more ambiguous. On the contrary they become for that all the clearer. And indeed because they are so clear they even tempt anyone who looks at them little by little towards the notion of *poetry*. Yes, reader, for my part I can see nothing there now except *poetry*. My mute mind is filled with a too blinding, utterly unreachable *poetry,* so that, far from being impatient, I come finally to a plateau of calmness akin to inebriation.

Encounter with Unavoidable Muck

Where this blob of muck lying on the road came from we can't exactly say. We can, however, readily call it muck. It's a very sticky granular substance mixed with a transparent liquid that glistens in the daylight and we can see that it isn't some elaborate fake wax model, because many minute air bubbles keep popping and disappearing on the surface. Its stink is so acid it nearly seems poisonous and so everyone is certainly entitled to turn away and cover his nose; even that public servant, the garbageman, might not be unconditionally required to remove it. To pretend, however, that it does not exist and to ignore the fact that such a thing is ever continuously being formed inside our bodies would be not only wholly unhygienic and harmful, but an abominable hypocrisy, and one that would make us lose sight of one important link in the structure of the world we live in.

Seen from a microscopic aspect, this thing would be reduced to molecules with a rightful place in a scientific inventory, not much dissimilar from other organic substances. Observed macroscopically, it possesses a certain humble function, within a well-established order, as one of the processes of biological metabolism and also of the food chain. A number of maggots, indeed, have taken up residence therein and, if we could judge it without any preconceptions, even its stench would not be necessarily so different from that of a certain kind of delicacy we sometimes eat.

But of course our physical senses are not so flexible as to be deceived by those lines of thought. We can't deny the fact that we maintain a sort of awe for this blob of muck until light and weather result in its disintegration, its particles reduced to dust in air that we unintentionally inhale. And it could be said that, in having this sort of awe for this thing in such a manner, our minds reveal their most unclarifiable depths.

Obsession with an Apple

You can't say it's red. It's an apple—not a color. You can't say it's round. It's not a shape but an apple. You can't say it's sour. It's not a taste but an apple. You can't say it's expensive. It's not a price—it's an apple. You can't say it's pretty. It isn't beauty—it's an apple. You can't classify it, because it's not a fruit but an apple.

It's a flowering apple, a fruit-bearing apple, an apple that trembles on a branch in the wind. It's a rain-beaten apple, a peckable apple, a pickable apple. It's an apple that falls to earth, an apple that rots. It's a seed-bearing apple, a budding apple, an apple that need not be called an apple. An apple that need not be an apple; an apple that may be an apple. Apple or not, one apple is all apples.

Jonathan, crab, golden, winesap, Fuji, Tsugaru apples. One apple. Three, five, a dozen apples. Fifteen pounds, twelve tons, two million tons of apples. Apples to be produced, apples to be transported. Apples to be weighed and packed and sold. Apples to be sprayed, digested, consumed. Apples to be annihilated. Apples! Apples? That one, that one there, that one over there.

That one there, there in the basket. That one falling off the table, that one transposed to canvas, that one to be baked in the oven. A child holds it and bites it. That one, there. However much it rots, however many are eaten, apples go on growing on trees and endlessly filling the stores, shining. Of what is an apple a replica? Of what time a replica?

We can't answer. It's just an apple. We can't ask. It's just an apple. We can't discuss it. Finally, it's nothing but an apple, even now ....

Contents of a Limited Edition of Poems Entitled, *A Model of the World*

for Irisawa Yasuo

This collection of poems will only begin to exist when the following items have been placed in a finite container. Official registration of the design is now being applied for. Not for sale.

1. Down. Picked up on the street. Probably sparrow breast down.
2. A spring. Made of brass. Approx.15mm wide, 50mm long.
3. A picture postcard. Sender's name illegible.
4. A piece of orange cellophane. Can be used for holding over the eye and looking at scenery.
5. A silicon rectifying chip. 1N34 or equivalent.
6. A stalk of bamboo. Known scientifically as *Phyllostachys Heterocycla* var. pubescence.
7. A paper airplane made of a page of any book of poems published in 1973.
8. A small handful of sand. Should be dry.
9. A wafer for wrapping a dose of powdered medicine. "Japanese Pharmacopoeia."
10. One-way ticket between Niubu and Higashi-Bifuka on the Biko Line of Japanese National Railways. Unpunched.
11. Something blue.
12. One death registration. Stamped by the office of Tokyo's Suginami Ward.
13. A jew's-harp.
14. A quantity of explosives sufficient to obliterate the book of poems in case of emergency. The reader must decide what an emergency is.
15. A pair of scissors to be used when item 4 is too large. Also usable for making item 7.
16. Something as yet unnamed. Though each of its elements is clearly named (a leaf of a coniferous tree, a marshmallow, a rusty one-inch nail, a liquid spray, a small-power UHF oscillator, and 300 grams of ground pork and beef, etc.) the thing in its totality is unnamable.
17. The groaning voices of people recorded on a C30 cassette tape.

18. A sealed old matchbox.
19. Something else blue.
20. A small and ceremonial object, something that resembles a pair of plain wooden chopsticks, or in fact the chopsticks themselves.
21. A small steel nickel-coated device for keeping item 2 coiled tight.
22. A heat-warped phonograph record. I don't mind that it was stolen.
23. A packet of sunflower seeds.
24. A section 6 of a map of Nagano Prefecture on a scale of 1/50,000. The copyright owner/publisher/printer is the Institute for Geographical Research. Surveyed in 1910, revised in 1937.
25. A fruit knife.
26. A comb. Worn with use.
27. A wooden toy top.
28. A red pencil. Used for crossing out rather than for writing, a kind of weapon to combat language.
29. *Ajinomoto* or *Inoichiban*.
30. Scraps of a comic strip from any paper. Any number of scraps.
31. A monument of limited significance to a certain person. Less than 5 kilograms.
32. Enough currency to buy item 10. Only in case it is lacking.
33. Erase item 6. An editorial emendation.
34. Soil necessary for growing 23, including rain and sunshine. That is, this book of poems can be made possible only if there are a certain number of unspecified readers to share in the making.
35. Time which makes 34 possible.
36. A calendar required for measuring 35.
37. An atomic bomb. One of the classical type. Should come with a simple manual of instructions.
38. Delete 14.
39. Because of the presence of 37, the possibility of this collection being realized is diminished considerably, so that in order to make poems possible we have to take the expedient step of making a catalog rather than collecting items themselves. So the following item is needed at once.
40. A small dictionary, preferably out of print.
41. Erase 27. Temporarily under repair because of the changing style of this catalog.

Definitions — 95

42. Cancel 5. Same reason.
43. Cross out 15. Same reason.
44. Remove 25. Same reason.
45. This item is missing.
46. Pieces of red and white cake in the shape of a chrysanthemum distributed free to primary school children on National Foundation Day, ca. 1940.
47. A whole spider web.
48. A mask.
49. A ball of crinkled yarn.
50. A song once prohibited by civil law and sung at least once.
51. Something whose use is unclear. Brown and glossy.
52. Something that was destroyed because of jealousy and later repaired and kept on record. Something, indecent yet still propagating, which makes salty water red. A flag that flutters in the breeze. A thumb print or a signature legally binding. Approx. 3 hectares of sweet potatoes. Saliva produced by a black girl during her whole life. A miniature painting of a slum handed down by several generations of artists.
59. The largest available piece of a meteorite.
60. In order to control the unavoidable burgeoning and acceleration of this catalog, we withhold items 1-59, including things erased, deleted, removed, crossed out and canceled. We omit describing the relative changes thus made on this collection of poems and on this catalog.
61. When this catalog is reproduced in printed matter of the 3rd class mail category, we should include a copy of the printed matter in this catalog after stitching all the pages both length-wise and width-wise with linen thread.
62. A container that can hold 61 and all withheld items.
63. We restore item 7.
61. Maintain enough air outside this container to get item 7 air-borne.
65. A set of application forms that would enable this cataloger to avoid all legal, artistic and moral responsibility for the catalog. This application should be made to unspecified readers.
66. We restore items 23, 34 and 35.

Revising the Directions to My House

'The girl shouted, "Look, Ali! Squirrel!" and dropping her fan, she became senseless.'
—from *Revising the Directions to My House*

The Marunouchi Subway Line is famous for its roundabout course through Myogadani, Ochanomizu, Tokyo, Ginza, Yotsuya and Shinjuku Stations, although the distance between Ikebukuro in Toshima Ward and Ogikubo in Suginami Ward, the two ends of the line, is only nine kilometers measured in a straight line. My house, unfortunately, is near Minami Asagaya, one stop before the Ogikubo end of the line. When you emerge from my station, you'll inevitably come out on to the sidewalk along Ome Avenue. If you walk east, you'll find the Suginami Post Office on the south side and then the Police Station; on the north side is the Ward Office. A little further on is a sporting goods store (on the south side). Turn right at that corner, leaving the Avenue.

Along the road you'll pass the Water Works. The road doesn't wind too much there and pretty soon you'll come to the Asagaya Housing Project, sort of down the hill. Also, fortunately, there's a tennis court along about the last fifty meters of the road. So, by turning left at the fork and left again at the pay phone down the street, you'll have gone about half away around the tennis court. (But the Tax Office is on the right side after you've made that second left.)

Then the way gets easier. When you come to a narrow cross road, take that and not the other one. You'll probably notice one or two common tobacconists, but you don't have to get lost at all here. There aren't any man-made lakes or cliffs around there, so there's practically nothing to worry about. You take the path through the cemetery and come out at a greengrocer's. That'll be your landmark.

As always there's a wine shop next door and a bakery; then a dentist's office, a paint store, a bookstore, a fruit stand.... It goes on like that for a while. On this north side of Ome Avenue the neighborhood gets more crowded and the road goes on to the Asagaya National Railway Station. Of course, you can also walk to my place from there.

Conditions of Being

forming a shallow depression as it slowly rises, extending obliquely and twisting, bending at acute angles and folding itself again and again—
    sometimes floating, constantly swelling a bit (the whole body flowing), always rising, rising, balancing for a moment and then gently contorting itself, now softly undulating, gliding—
opening unnoticed, closing up the next moment, the surface now extending on to the underside, then gracefully turning over, (explosively converging), growing soft again, popping up, cramping, solidifying, melting, trembling, quietly stagnating, twitching,
    (crinkling up) and yet in utter silence—
    a force from beyond, a force producing a force here, force struggling with force, wriggling as though caught in a forcenet, expanding endlessly because of force, never severed, and creating through its irregular movement a strange rhythm, and aimlessly—
    (seeming to come full circle and not losing its direction)
    There is no microscope, nor macroscope. A cradle of flesh inside a cradle of a planet, we live in vertigo under the blessing of infinity.

The End Result of a Perfect System

One tree leaf is the end-result of a perfect system. Its veins are purely functional and yet their pattern suggests that they wish to be interpreted by us. (We could almost say that they are written down.) Those who read them as a prophetic book should die in an abbey; those who read them as a blueprint will develop cancer; those who read them as a map will get lost in the woods; and those who read them as bones should spend a long autumn day singing.

Even if this is not an attractive temptation, and we read nothing into the pattern of veins, we nevertheless can't escape a human viewpoint and it is evident that this perfect system has shut down already and ended in a place far removed from human eyes. Even the slimmest tree perfectly embodies this fact. Not by its leaves alone but by a twig reaching toward the sky and roots feeling their dark way, and even by the way the tree feebly withers.

A Personal Opinion about Gray

There has never been a perfectly white white. Even in a perfect white an imperceptible trace of black is present and that is invariably the very nature of whiteness itself. White does not regard black as hostile; instead, white produces black because of its whiteness; white promotes black. From the very onset of whiteness, white points toward blackness.

Whatever tones of gray it may undergo in its long journey toward black, white never ceases being white until the instant it turns into complete black. Even if white is violated by such non-white elements as shadow, dullness or absorption of light, white keeps shining behind a mask of gray. White dies in an instant. In that instant, white vanishes without a trace and complete black is born. But—

There has never been a perfectly black black. In a black that completely lacks radiance, an imperceptible trace of white is present, like a gene, and that is invariably the nature of blackness itself. From the very onset of blackness, black points toward whiteness ....

Observations on Fun in the Water

First, wet footprints disappeared; then cute dimples and large eyes disappeared. Pink nails, curly black hair and kneecaps disappeared, and then, in this way, the blue sky also instantly vanished, as did flowers, and words. Of course soldiers disappeared. This is to say that everything, from the certain to the uncertain, disappeared.

To talk about this situation as 'the disappearance of everything' is a stereotyped sort of expression used by lazy poets, and yet in fact this 'everything disappeared' has also disappeared, which means that ' "everything disappeared" has disappeared' has also disappeared, but in the next moment, before we had time to indulge in this word-play, lively trout appeared. No sooner had we thought about these things than a leather briefcase, owner unknown, statute books, and 2:13 p.m. appeared; and at the same time lovers began to show up. Wet footprints appeared again in a flash and a bared belly with its navel coiling in the middle, and Miss S's cheerful smile (5 years and 5 months old) also appeared.

Detailed Description of the Last Day of the World

Green apples fall from branches on a windless day. Grazing sheep begin to bleat and go on bleating all night. Squeaking doors grow light as feathers. Book-marks fall from closed books and then all at once inside the brand new opera house voices are unable to reach the boxes. Cracks naturally creep across stained glass windows. But it is unbearable that children stop crying. Now ants, unable to return to their hill, get lost in the grass and the tuning forks of tuning fork-clocks start sounding a half-note higher; socks drop no matter how often you pull them up, table legs are paralyzed, and wallpaper sprouts rashes. But the feeling of jealousy doesn't go away at all but intensifies more and more. And because nothing can be decided, heads of households' stomachs harden into wooden sheets, sink, and take the shapes of ships' hulls. By the time the supply of coffee beans is exhausted the Jack of Hearts begins staring straight ahead, camels in the zoo amble out into the street. Stars sidle up to each other as as if chair-ridden, while iron sculptures are remodeled into giant hammers. *Mandala* buddhas go up-river, their skirts hiked up, and pregnant women, ignorant of what is happening, line up. Every single event is a foreboding of the next and as always medals go on being awarded, but gradually the world's details lose their contours and their peculiar stenches.

The spirals have gone straight, straight lines have all gone limp, and sag; circles are distorted, and parallel lines have turned away from one another. We would find this laughable but our muscles and skin have separated. Something like pieces of tin keep falling from the sky. Shadows of wisdom never yet realized come across an idiot's face. Air is swallowed in a vacuum. All living languages, oral or written, merge into a circular cry and when these languages eddy in the gentle embrace of silence, a single dandelion seed is floating vainly near our cheeks, trying to reach the ground.

Pseudo-Anatomical Self-Portrait

I ate strawberries. I have first molars capped with gold. I saw the first foliage of a tree I can't identify. I have irises. I drove a nail into plywood. I have biceps. I repeated a song passage that I half-remembered. I have sublingual glands. I smelled the perfume of a woman I passed in the air on Nakasugi Street. I have glans. I wrote a few words with the aid of a dictionary. I have thenars and hypothenars. Because I don't know what is important I keep on writing 'I ... I ... I ...' I have a temporal lobe.

    I am unable to know exactly what I am. In spite of that, I contain phenylpyruvic acid. I keep on discovering myself, a part of me, delighted over my friend's misery, and for such mental construct the sacroiliac within me is partly responsible. I have Meissner's tactile corpuscles, by means of which I can perceive the sweaty body of a drunk who leans on me in the train; but I don't want to acknowledge that his neuroglias are the same as mine. I won't be able to avoid being self-imprisoned until I die. This fact makes me slightly dizzy. I have a modiolus which is related, through earth's gravity, to the unknown inter-stellar substance. I shall someday be burned in an incinerator, leaving behind only a thyroid cartilage.

A Note on Ritual

Lift both your arms horizontally for the sake of the space you belong to. Keep breathing calmly for the sake of the time in which you are. Spit, so that you can stand on your scorn. Close your eyes, so that you will become wise through awe.

Touch your lips to water to demonstrate men's thirst. Walk across briars as one hypocrite. Burn incense, share the air with others. Ring a bell as a burden upon silence. Don't follow custom. Improvisation is allowed to you, but don't tell fortunes and don't prophesy.

Don't wear a feather of a dead bird, but bedeck yourself with uprooted weeds. Don't acquire disciples or build too high an altar. Wish for nothing; just moan wordlessly.

Pound the earth with your fist as proof of your obedience to the universe. Hide your face with your palm in order to approach the dead. Jump three times for your happy fellow-humans. So that you may not waste your abuse, say your name.

Bleed, be self-sacrificial; but never die. Survive, wave a five-colored flag like a nonchalant conjurer.

Will the Landscape Flow out of the Frame?

The artist has painted a picture which, however, has come out quite different from what's before him. It is, moreover, quite different from what he and his heart originally intended. What you see in the foreground looks like a small bottle of ordinary eye drops. In the middle you see the sky and in the back something like animal footprints. The tone is uniformly sepia-like so that the overall impression is that of the variegated grain of a thick oak board.

No one can specify where the scene is or even dare to say what it's about. But it fails to be in any way abstract; nor does it correspond to any imaginable image. This picture cannot be expected to hang on any kind of wall in any kind of room, but neither it nor its painter should therefore be punished. The painting, then, is like an accidental, and therefore sincere, window opening up on the innumerable things of this world, and what we see through this window is forever concealed.

The frame of this artifact, done so carefully by a perhaps reticent craftsman, is the only grounds for guessing at the painting,'s value, but nobody guarantees that it will not flow out of its frame.

An Example of an Essay Containing an Open Window

A window is open. The open window is connected to the scenery by a rope of twisted wind. No, I observe the window only partially because my glance tends to focus towards the outside. No, the open window is colored with an ochre paint that continually pales. No, the open window lets the faint sound of the outside world come into the room, borne on the air flowing in to fill in the opening. No, the open window registers, by the very state of its being open, the action of the man who opened it a few minutes ago. No, the open window for half a century has modestly displayed the skills of craftsmen.

No, the open window is one trivial illusion. Any description of the window's details is nothing but crude material to satisfy the speaker's words. No, the open window is one useless idea and it creates a sense of momentary unstable solidarity between one person and several others. No, the open window symbolizes all the windows in the world that are open at this moment and which we have no way of measuring or counting. No, the open window is one of those oscillating images that are continually falling from reality into metaphors. No, the open window will never be destroyed even in the most delirious written context. No, the open window is meaningless. No, the open window transmits hatred. An ant is crawling on the window frame. A window is open.

Naming Hidden Names

The first name was shouted in horror. The second, because of shock, was not voiced and the third was the moaning of a beast. The fourth name was a mere sigh, the fifth a voiceless whisper in the darkness and the sixth is now a taboo. The seventh was indistinguishable from unhappy laughter, the eighth a curse, the ninth an amorous whisper, and the tenth foreshadowed castes. The eleventh and twelfth names were of course abusive swearing, and the thirteenth name was borrowed from another. The fourteenth was idle onomatopoeia and the fifteenth died as soon as it was called. The sixteenth name was not repeated and the seventeenth drove a man to death, while the eighteenth interrupted it, and the nineteenth name was only nominal.

Now the twentieth was the name for everything under the sun, the twenty-first the name of nothing at all and the twenty-second was easily uttered by everyone. The twenty-third was pleasing, like sleep, the twenty-fourth recited in halfdreaming, while the twenty-fifth pointed towards the beyond, and the twenty-sixth name was at last anonymous .... So with the twenty-seventh name, a name became a word for the first time, and the name begot a name, the name named a name. and the name became a new word by denying a name, as it went on multiplying, like cancer cells, until every possible name in the world wound up being written in a dictionary. And all the prior twenty-six names which were spared inclusion in the dictionary are buried somewhere near our shin bones, without any suitable sounds or transcriptions.

'NA'

At 11:42 p.m., on October 26, I write 'na' in *hiragana*. 'Na' means, first, every *hiragana* character 'na' in whatever has been written in the Japanese language; second, 'na' means the illusions of things and objects which the sound 'na' could refer to, and all the associations that arise from those illusions. That is to say, 'na' contains the possibility of beginning with 'na' and spreading out to the entire world. The third meaning is as a record of my act of having written 'na'; the fourth meaning is the meaninglessness inherent in all of those things.

At 11:45 p.m., October 26, I erase the 'na' I have written. The space where the 'na' used to be means a denial of all four meanings above, and also the impossibility of that denial; that is, if I did not describe the fact of having written and then erased 'na', those acts would not exist for other people and therefore those acts would be lost. But if I do describe them I would be unable to deny the 'na' in any way whatsoever.

'Na' thus has come to exist. At 11:47 p.m., October 26, I cannot betray the form of my existence. I can't transcend language. Not even by a single 'na.'

Darkness in the Throat

The following poetic exercises inevitably involve the human body and the natural voice but does not take the form of script, document or dreams and the reason I publish it is that the vividness of the bodies and voices of that particular time and place lured a language out of me.

I conveyed to the actors of 'Group Sonnet' the outline of the following things by means of incoherent utterances, gestures and verbal imitations, and though they were perplexed they produced in the air a temporary illusion via their transient arms, legs throats and lips. All these things caused me to shiver as ordinary language could never do.

The following mass of printed letters, however, will be a great deal different from the actual events.

A Caricature of Birds and Beasts

Several men and women are standing, either at dawn or during broad daylight. The place is also arbitrary. If your purpose is enjoyment, the place could be somewhere on a wasteland; if you want spectators it could be staged. The actors needn't be professionally trained performers. And maybe they are not themselves. They might be ourselves.

They seem at first silent. Listening, however, you might hear the various sounds emitted by their bodies, such as circulation of blood, throbbing of hearts, breathing, and the sounds of digestive organs; and among these sounds you might hear the momentum of bodies ready to utter something.

Their lips slightly part and there can be heard soft whispering sounds almost like breathing. These sounds may be, first of all, the murmuring of timid but sensitive birds that perceived the rising of sounds beyond the distant massed clouds, or nasal voices of some still blind baby beasts that are groping for their mothers' nipples.

The volume and kinds of sounds gradually increase until they finally reach, ideally, a level of plenitude that includes all earthly fauna. But the actors are not necessarily required to produce realistic imitations of every single bird's or beast's voice.

In the case of hens, cows, sheep, dogs and cats, for instance, it would be natural in principle to imitate or broadly reproduce. But in the case of other phyla, classes, orders, families, genus or species of birds and beasts, all possible sounds except human voices will be imaginatively reproduced. But although odd indeed those utterances may be, they naturally can't match up to the voices of creatures that have been on earth for millions of years.

After a few minutes the voices gradually abate until at last they are so faint as to be nearly inaudible, and yet they keep on sounding into the next phase.

A Moaning Fugue

A man and woman are standing some distance apart, not facing each other. They seem unaware of each other's existence. Perhaps their eyes are quite naturally closed.

We can see their chests heave slowly and their shoulders rise and fall. In the stillness we can hear a faint sound. This sound, heard off and on, gives us the impression as of a floating in the air, but soon it becomes evident that it is the moaning of a man and a woman.

The two moaning voices, with a very slow and irregular cycle, occasionally break apart and occasionally entangle as they advance. This could be described as musical volume ranging from pianissimo to mezzoforte, always cautiously controlled by diminuendo and crescendo.

The moaning seems to be trying to convey physical pain but is also an unconscious expression of sexual pleasure. At times, however, the voices might be heard as the releasing of a profound anxiety that cannot otherwise be overcome.

Anyway, the moaning is too profound to suggest any single situation. Although it is clear that the voices arise from two human throats, they sound as though they are some superhuman feelings blown by an invisible presence using human bodies as its whistle.

(Perhaps for the sake of keeping the moaning from being merely lyrical, several human shadows squatting behind the couple may sometimes give very ordinary coughs.)

Pointillism

Here each person achieves what could be called a unit of human utterance, apparently distinct from the voices of birds and beasts, although still themselves meaningless. Even so, the process is never smooth but even grotesquely clumsy, and earnest as well.

For those new voices are not willed into being by each person. At least for the first brief period they well up from within in a way even a bit as comical as a hiccup.

To utter even a single orderly sound by using vocal cords, tongue, teeth and palate, never consciously used before, is an action that meets an unexpectedly great resistance. Some try to spit out sounds by stammering while others try to give sounds by straining their muscles.

Yet as they keep on struggling with these rising voices each person unconsciously learns to control them and proceeds further to create his own sounds. Each reaches this state without help, but soon he learns to project to others these voices that he has mastered.

This is an innocent game. Though it signifies nothing, voices charged with a human passion that seeks companionship flit about like balls in space.

These voices consist mostly of one single sound but heard within a group of people the sounds also sound like part of the system of an unknown language. Now it seems that everyone present enjoys the variety of new voices by aurally distinguishing the various sounds and pronouncing them.

Calling a Name

Names were created when sounds and objects were connected. This is not to trace the origin of languages in explanatory terms. The sort of shock people felt when a theretofore meaningless sound like 'eye' became associated with an actual eye someone pointed at may remain here on this ambiguous occasion (though I don't know why).

Such names as 'eye', 'tooth', 'ear' or 'hand', however, will never appear with ecstasy or a refreshing feeling but are created through pain or loathing. They will be accompanied by the symptom of serious stammering, and each individual as these words are used becomes again a prisoner of something uncontrollable, but that does not last long.

People quickly grow accustomed to those names and by giving names to things they begin discovering the world. They are then overmastered by child-like enthusiasm, astonishment and awe, and everyone speaks to everyone else the names of bodily parts, clothes and belongings.

Each name is carefully pronounced and even lyrically repeated. This is how names rapidly mushroom. In other words people begin hungrily calling out the various names of as many things around them as they can see and of as many people as there are in the world.

The kind of ritualistic raving that began with the naming of visible concrete objects could not but become abstract and migrate into the realm of imagination. Name summoned up name, association summoned up association, and no one saw or heard the actual world any more, but persisted with the vocabulary of his own inner world.

Before they have time to consider whether a reality actually corresponds to those names, they continually call out name after name. Those names no longer function; they go out of circulation. Names become strangely magical things, like prayers to Buddha, and finally even the act of calling names seems to have been buried in fatigue.

'a' and 'i'

The first two extremely simple phonemes of the Japanese syllabary are rediscovered in a flood of names. When the process of indiscriminately calling out the names of every possible object and idea and mixed reality and unreality results in the process being found unbearably empty, people become babies again and suddenly begin mouthing 'a' and 'i' as some sort of social fashion.

They say nothing save 'a' and 'i'. They pronounce these in various ways, as in admiration or in love, and try to place every emotion there is into those sounds, as if they were partly mute.

With 'a' and 'i' as their sole language, they speak to others and expect a reply in the impoverished vocabulary of 'a' and 'i.' In some sense they are ascetics, like mendicant monks begging alms in 'a' and 'i.' In a wave they are like a group of morbid madmen receiving group therapy.

Villagers unrelated to them or passers-by or the audience (if we envision a play) or even we ourselves—do these people humiliate them who try to speak to them? Or do they try somehow to speak with them in a broken language?

Anyway, after some time each of them must live in solitude and be left alone. In that final moment of disappointment the sounds 'a' and 'i' will merge on the lips of one person and give birth to the Japanese word 'love' (*ai*). That person, however, is no longer able in his own mind to grasp the reality of that word.

Perhaps he or she was on the verge of grasping meaning for the first time ever. Perhaps he or she was about to utter for the very first time a sentence.

But that word can only slip into an amorphous universe of infinite human language which is being written here and now in this very moment. A few men and women who gathered briefly in time and space have now dispersed and the distant sound of human noises can be heard as if to prove that there is no such thing as complete silence anywhere.

Afterword

Afterword

The critic who would come to some of the poems of Tanikawa Shuntaro wielding a set of logical procedures and rational terms drawn from Western philosophy would be ill-advised. To be sure, the poems (62 *Sonnets,*) here and there invite and yield to logical analysis and, as readily as any poems may be said to do, often lend themselves to paraphrase and explication in terms familiar to most Western critics; but to state only that much is by no means to suggest that Western critical terms and methods are sufficient for a fuller understanding of those sixty-two poems. Just so, ambiguity, inner contradiction, opaqueness, or illogic are to be considered characteristics that often positively enrich Tanikawa's poems rather than as defects the eradication of which would improve the poems. Nor, for another example, is the mixing of tenses a bogy either for Tanikawa or for Japanese poetry generally. All these will regularly upset a translator but are of little or no concern to a writer or a reader or an auditor of poetry in Japanese.

If upon careful readings of Tanikawa's poems the critic decides that indeed they reject philosophic scepticism according to which there is no such thing as valid knowledge, that they develop the realist's view that things in fact exist apart from our minds, and that they also affirm (or at least assume) the phenomenalist's view that there must be some ultimate reality beyond the superficial forms of 'real things,' of which, however, we can have no knowledge, then the critic will have neatly pigeon-holed Tanikawa (assuming, of course, that the points of view apparent in the poem nicely coincide with the poet's personal points of view): no pure sceptic, he is at once a realist and a phenomenalist. Insofar as the poems do not unequivocally posit a reality that is entirely dependent upon our minds, Tanikawa is not an idealist. If we find him alternating *dos-a-dos*, with Kant, Spencer, Descartes, Spinoza and Leibniz, while avoiding Locke, Berkeley and Hume, we have not discovered much, because, although we beg a serious question by assuming that the poems' ideas are also the poet's personal ones, the system of any one philosopher never comes into play in any poem, ideas and terms not relevant to or at least characteristic of Western philosophic systems do appear in some of the poems, and the objects under consideration, after all, are not philosophic essays but lyric poems. They are poems, moreover, which far from having any necessity to answer to the criteria imposed by logic or pure mathematics, themselves, create at least some of the standards by which they are to be judged. If the critic merely tries to squeeze and shove Tanikawa's poems into his own ready-made Western critical boxes, he will significantly fail.

In some sense rational discourse about Tanikawa's poems breaks down if the critic abandons the familiar analytical tools. The necessity of their employment in critical investigation is something beyond doubt, but their limitations quickly emerge when the critic comes up against a kind of emotional burden in the poems that a sensitive Japanese reader perhaps has no problem 'understanding' but that an American or English sensibility is hard put to handle and that a translator has in part to (mis)manage such that sufficiently clear English obtains. To the extent that the poems' ideas and emotional powers are similar to or at least comprehensible to the Western critic's, well and good. The poems are discussable. Enter an element with an especially Japanese flavor, however, and discussion screeches to a halt. One could recall in passing that sustained rational philosophizing in any field of endeavor in Japan is quite unusual. Treatises there are (such as Ki no Tsurayuki on poetry and Zeami on No) but there is nothing like a Japanese Aristotle, an Aquinas, a Kant, or a Whitehead; no Horace, Castelvetro, Dryden, or Crane. Those traditions of discourse never blossomed because logical structures and rational analysis were not uppermost on the scale of Japanese religious or esthetic values; no demand, no supply. If in the utter absence of ideas in poems one is looking at nonsense verse, of course Japanese poetry has always been a sensible poetry, but the burden of very much of it from as early as we know it is carried rather in the heart than in the mere head (the latter certainly being one aspect of the former in the word 'kokoro'). Except certain literary trends in Japan in the last century or so and we may safely claim that Japanese poets and readers prefer emotional richness, developed in simple or in complex ways, to *all* other possible poetic achievements. In England, poets as similar and dissimilar as John Donne and George Herbert achieve intense emotional effects on the strength, in part, of the ideas or 'arguments' of their poems—poems which are carried for eight, ten, twelve, fourteen, or even many more lines, and those, compared to the Japanese lines, long ones. You will not derive much intellectual meat from waka or haiku; nor from a lot of modern Japanese poetry either, in which the emotional atmosphere is important no matter how slight the 'argument.' The longer traditional forms died out, save for renga, which at all events is a special case not of course to be compared with such long forms as the *Iliad,* the *Divine Comedy, Paradise Lost* or *The Prelude,* architectonic literary structures of which there are no Japanese counterparts. The poets aimed at acute emotional intensity in their shockingly shallow wells of three or seven or, it may be, fifteen lines. 'Great ideas' are not meant to leap out of a mere mouthful of syllables. But the fine haiku poets did not need to build great ideas; they had other resources and ends which when handled expertly would leave the author or reader afloat on a sustaining sea of emotion. For the author or reader thus afloat, literary criticism is irrelevant, which is not to demean criticism but only to suggest that it has little or no place in the presence of Japanese sensibility. It was ever the aim of the Japanese poet—it is Tanikawa's ambition, as well—to impress the reader less with his cleverness with words than to approach as directly, as closely to the bare experience as possible; not to tell you how hot the stove is but to place it against your finger.

Certainly a Western critic would be able to investigate a haiku by Buson, to enquire into its discrete parts, its purpose, its shape, and its effect, and to ask how it is different from what it is not. That set of inductive and analytic questions, however, only partially responds to Buson's haiku. Among Japanese the basic job of work is the work of feeling, the sustaining of the emotion(s) effected by the poem, this carried on quietly, inside. What here is true of the Japanese is equally true of the Westerner. Yet now the latter will want to go on and figure out what happened and why. It is precisely this task that a Japanese will find uninteresting or downright boring, and possibly superfluous, arguing—if pushed—that the poem asks no analysis but only that one open his heart to it. It is fair to say that many a Western reader of haiku wants to establish an armchair philosophy around a haiku; he is the same observer who will find a moral in an ant's industriousness. By the same token, many a Japanese reader is unprepared to appreciate the challenges presented by, for instance, Pope's *Essay on Man.* Nor are all Japanese readers expert or avid, any more than their Western peers are; in this context, however, the subject is not so much audience expertise as cultural orientation, literary expectation, and critical focus.

Some conclusions can properly be drawn about Tanikawa's poems. It is necessary only to remember to let one's critical schema take one as far as it will and, for the rest of it, to judge the poems as one finds them whether the schema is useful or not.

It remains to enter one final demurrer about the essay that follows; to wit, that while one does suspect that the ideas found in *62 Sonnets* are also chiefly to be found in all of Tanikawa's poems across three decades, the present essay looks almost exclusively at *62 Sonnets,* both its bits and pieces and as a whole in the impression it leaves. Restless or restlessly inventive, Tanikawa has been almost at pains never to repeat himself formally in any of his books of poems, so that although favorite words, phrases, and concepts survive across the length of his publications career he remains, so to speak, untrue to form. Every collection is a new step for his mankind. The demurrer, then, is that in writing about Tanikawa's poems I cannot pretend to be speaking about Japanese poetry or even about all of Tanikawa s poems. Reference is made to other of his books, but here I speak of one book, and only of four facets of that: Time as Real and Unreal, Nature, Language, and Knowledge *A Posteriori* and *A Priori.*

FOUR FACETS OF 62 SONNETS

1[a] *Time as Real*: If Time did not exist someone would have to invent it. Someone did. We do not now gauge Time's slippage, elapsing, flight, or amount by water trickling, by strings of sand cascading, by shadows sliding, or lately, not even so much by hands sweeping, as by black dots flicking and digits changing. *Chronos* is an imposition from without and cultural overlays like milliseconds and half-lives and lustra are not universals; nor do New Year's Days, where they exist, all occur simultaneously. For Time and Time schemes are teaching devices and social contrivances that nurture and measure national histories as surely as they measure anything else. Geopolitical though it is, down at the grass roots Time personal varies from culture to culture, the age of a baby born in one country not necessarily reckoned in the same way as the age of a baby born in another; and the older of your twins is not necessarily the older of mine, though both infants emerged first of the two sets. Time hangs on how you count, what you count, and where you begin counting. High noon to a Saudi Arabian and to an Icelander means something different. What is longevity to a giant or to a dwarf? Perhaps we are looking not at Time at all but at Time schemes, all of them relative to historical cultures.

The living process consists in atomic relocations, in lump-sum fashion to the naked eye and in rapid succession to the equipped eye. The process may be blind in the sense that, so far at least, we have no *a posteriori* knowledge that these relocations have any value, since value and its judgment themselves derive from religious or philosophic systems which are as man-made as Time. One unproved assumption cannot validate another.

Time as a cultural yardstick does indeed exist in numerous forms, of which if Time is any indication we have not yet seen the last. 'Many moons' preceded birth certificates and where certificates were irrelevant, as in the case of bones, along came the carbon-dating process, which is itself less accurate than subsequent methods. In fact isn't pedigree a function of Time? And where does a millisecond belong in something as engulfing as 'the Bronze Age?' Time does not exist. What exists are systems for measuring it. If you invent the thing there is every rational justification for inventing the instrumentality to record or measure whatever the thing's properties are said to be (though they also do not exist). At times, no doubt, the instrumentation preceded the concept, the latter born of the former, just as a shattered windshield might suggest a radiating sunburst pattern to an artist working in stained glass. There is a Time for everything under the sun, including a Time for man to take his cue not from nature but from a broken windshield. In a reversal of Plato on the point, the quasi-eternal form called the sun comes to be three removes from the reality of the stained glass window.

Time systems are real. In sonnet 4 Sunday and Monday appear, the passage of Time indicated by the passage of clouds. Or is *that* what Time is, or is to be measured by: the passage of something else (clouds) that is by its nature as close to unreal as the real can get? In this poem there is a sequencing from sunny to cloudy to sunny, and then to a 'next':

> Sunday again,
> and Monday's cloudy again
> and then turns sunny;
> and who knows what's next?

This is common sense reckoning, awareness of the passage of Time in gross lots—until, in the next lines, the poet decides that Time is an imaginative figment and that what is urgently present is solely "today":

> I remember nothing but today.
> Death would be 'today'
> and living is intensely 'today.'

Yet the lines while seeming to allude to the vagaries or the imperfection of memory in fact point to the poet's notion of Time as both real and unreal. Its reality, expressed abstractly in sonnet 4, and his awareness of it, are dressed in helpful concrete details in 5:

> So this is life, after all?
> People swarm the sun-swept morning streets;
> children pass by, laughing like sparrows;
> illusions whirl along like wind.

In the next stanza, however, he returns to the felt presence of poem 4's 'today':

> Today sings before eternity,
> its song both younger
> and more abstruse.
> It sings more eternally than eternity.

And then comes another implicit and explicit denial that Time exists, in sonnet 6:

> I have no time or place to start from.
> I just live,
> killing my days,
> my heart alone overflowing.

Apparently Time does and does not exist; or one 'kills' those units built into the system called Time. Tanikawa's heart is filled to overflowing by his awareness of 'today's' events and underlying that awareness is a sense that Time progresses (he does not choose to speak of Time as a flowing, because later he will state plainly that Time does not flow). But flow, progress, march, or fly, Time is and is not. Paradoxically Time is in the world but not of it, whereas Tanikawa himself is both in *and* of the world—at least at this point in the sequence. By what he is deeply moved (his heart is overflowing), if indeed he knows, he does not yet say. The sky is overcast, morning is yet aborning, and he seems both optimistic and content while possessed of (or by) a profound yearning.

It is in poem 8 that he introduces the denial that Time does not flow:

> What is does not flow.
> What comes and goes knows
> nothing but this present moment.

Up to this point one might have suspected that Time is fluid, particularly because from the beginning and continuing throughout the sequence clouds are tirelessly forming and reforming, and coming and going, and clouds would be a standard metaphor for Time as a flowing. In Western thought clouds are taken, also, to signify the imagination or daydreaming ('his head is in the clouds') while fog, mist or haze signify bewilderment ('his mind is in a fog'). It is probably safe enough to say that for the Japanese clouds and fog-mist-haze suggest unreality, transience, or the unreliability of perceived phenomena. Now all at once in poem 8, lines 9-11 state that Time is present only in the present (there are implications in this notion for language or its usage; for instance, tenses are vitiated and one is left with no compunction to conjugate verbs consistently, since only the present is thought to exist). There is no chronology, no retreat and no advance, and no circularity appears implicit either. There is only the here-now, and that occurring not in a *series* of here-nows but once only. This is not an unfamiliar view of Time, although 'killing time' would appear to assume a biding and biding a flowing process. What then Tanikawa kills as he waits is not Time as a fluid process; he kills what is and *only* is: here-now. Patiently or impatiently, he waits (even those adverbs denote 'calm' or 'troubled' endurance and 'endurance' implies the passage of Time). It would seem impossible to escape from Time insofar as we are users of (the English) language.

We may ultimately conclude that Tanikawa is ambivalent. In seeking to return to a Timelessness he is acknowledging that he does now inhabit a sphere of the Timely and the Timed. But ambivalence is no cause for embarrassment. He is, let us say, a mystic pragmatist who in the end—by sonnet 62—may have become a pragmatic mystic.

Sufferance? Calm and troubled endurance? He experiences discomfort and uneasiness in having to be a child of Time when his origins, he believes, lie in Timelessness. 'If I could only forget Time,' he argues, I could possibly escape its clutches.' Poem 13 reads:

> When I believe in this moment in all its richness,
> even though I am aware of death,
> I am free.

Thus to give oneself means to abandon memories and dreams (of the past and the future), and to attend alertly to present consciousness. Cares also vanish ('the world dies away') and hence he becomes free of both anxiety and Time, the one caused by the other. With past and future eliminated, bad memories as well as good and fearful visions as well as cheerful are disspelled, and he is becalmed. One is reminded of I.A. Richards' notions of about half-a-century ago (Cf. *Principles of Literary Criticism,* 1924; and *Practical Criticism,* 1929) that, as distinct from pure mathematics but at least relatable to natural sciences, poetic utterance is the self's way of organizing conflicting impulses and expressing these so that a saner selfhood might materialize. Richards the empiricist was caught up in a struggle to save Poetry's face and place in its confrontation with other pretenders to the throne of theoretic truth.

Tanikawa does not, withal, escape Time either in person or in the poems, and in poem 29 we find him still set on living in the moment if, ironically, not for it:

> Today returns;
> yesterday is a blur;
> I can't imagine the shape of tomorrow.

He is at least partly "free" in these lines and since there is no evidence of psychopathology or any other shred of disease in the poems we are able to conclude that he is, one might have thought, in some sense religiously committed to honoring his portion of life in the here-now; to using his capacities to the full in order to investigate and report and praise. He is not a hedonist; not a *tabula rasa* on which here-now scribbles graffiti. In poem 31 he states, 'I bear witness in the midst of a festival.' And a few lines later:

> I read a book of time.
> Everything is recorded there —and therefore nothing.
> I bombard yesterday with questions.

He is clearly an autonomous moral agent at work in a world of Time, appreciatively sensible of the world's body while hoping fervently to participate in the world's soul. By dint of emotional openness and intellectual curiosity, and recognizing hence that he has the property of extension, he sallies into the world, no righteous Don Quixote but a sensitively lyric Sancho. He senses the world in five ways and then, in 37:

> I go back into myself.
> No one's there.
> Where do I come from?
> I was born of infinity.
>
> I'd like to be everywhere at once, like light.
>
> . . . .
>
> [but am] unable to become even a mild breeze.

Here is the young poet whose heart perhaps goes out to an 'O altitudo' but who despite his youth and high aspirations is securely enough the honest journeyman pilgrim-as-poet to know that:

> People have to use up love,
> say, in songs or sweat;
> or change it into other forms.

And ever faithfully attendant upon the world's beauty in the arena of Time, he states, in poem 12:

> I shall never sing again
> of yesterday's undoubted happiness,
> of tomorrow with its promise of sorrow,
> nor of today, skies clear to the point of vanity.

Isn't human life in these lines regarded as a lovely stand-off? Observing that the world is beautiful, he is tugged at by a Time that is remoreseless and unforgiving yet against which he does not rail or write scampish poems. Echoes of Dylan Thomas resound: 'Time ... in the mercy of his means ... Let me hail and climb ... held me green and dying/Though I sang in my chains like the sea.' Man is ravaged by Time, however gently, however slowly; and Time will tell.

He plucks off the petals of that daisy Time, 'It is, it's not, it is, it's not ....' Did anything ever so powerfully (non-) exist? If this is an oxymoron, so be it, for some evidence suggests that Tanikawa's ambivalence and paradoxes are sustainable and not just a result of fuzzy thinking; besides, we are here reading a sonnet sequence rather than a systematic essay about Time. (62 *Sonnets* are intense lyric poems, each of them fourteen lines. Most of the poems can stand alone while all of them gain in coherence from being read as a sequence. The book is probably the most sustained poetic investigation of Time in Japanese literary history.) Thus we may expect, allow and welcome contradiction and indecisiveness, taking these, in acceptable Japanese fashion, as qualities that rather enrich than simplify and shut down the discussion. (As is well known, ancient Japanese poems permit multiple readings such that in effect what we would ordinarily call one poem may be interpreted and translated in several ways, and some of those contradictory or unrelated. The Japanese do not always highly value logical clarity or intellectual coherence and will enthusiastically sacrifice anything for the sake of emotional depth or human affections.) Far from being a simpleton or a wide-eyed dreamer, Tanikawa is philosophically a hard-thinking, complex, and squinting dreamer, nobody's fool and not Time's tool either. 'There is a time for all things under the sun,' as including a Time to affirm as well as to deny the simple past, the simple present, and the simple future.

1b *Time as Unreal*: Judged by direct and indirect references in *62 Sonnets*, Tanikawa is more often aware of than unaware of Time (which may well be the usual state of affairs with most people; not that we think continually in terms of long stretches of Time; yet we are always conscious or half-conscious of hours elapsed since the last pill was taken, the approaching hour for the evening television newscast, the minutes gone by since we started the washing machine, and the days that lie between now and Valentine's Day). Time eats at us, if you will, nibbling the leaves of our lives as if it were a silkworm, and the poet is almost always conscious of this. For him the test of Time's fell weight is the extent to which he feels unburdened when in some odd moment he manages to forget Time and is for a moment suddenly exalted. Indeed the momentary experience is virtually epiphanal:

> My heart removed me to a height
> from which I looked down on time. (14)
>
> Feigning ignorance,
> I package time and send it
> in the direction of yesterday.
>
> Yet some things I can't get rid of.
> I cling to those and find suddenly
> a new beginning. (17)
>
> I keep on walking
> through the expansion of things.
>
> ....
>
> I stop looking and all at once
> I begin to live. (19)

> And yet our joy is in trusting in
> ...
> ...
> ... a heart beyond forms. (22)

And then, eleven poems later, losing himself, he finds himself:

> I tried getting closer
> but backed off again;
> tried backing off
> but again drew near.
>
> Always in utter self-forgetfulness
> my mind gestures fantastically.
> In trying to find the mind's order
> I get lost in the human woods.
>
> My excuse is always the joy of life.
> My love is leaping
> and is at times indifferent to everything.
>
> The blue sky is not a roof but an old well.
> I threw myself in,
> only to be reborn. (33)

The subject or the impetus for this sonnet strikes me as indefinite. What he tries to approach and retreat from, what or why, are unclear. What are the mind's fantastic gesturings? Just what is the relation of his 'excuse,' 'the joy of life,' to his occasional indifference to 'everything'? What sort of ecstasy—we presume it is not a despairing act—is it to throw himself into the 'blue sky'? Some of these statements are apparently contradictory; none is patently clear; and all have a few conceivable meanings. The poem delivers just a sufficient amount of sense to prevent the reader from being distracted by the sense and to keep him close to the swarming, seething emotional depths created by that bare sense. Doesn't Dylan Thomas frequently manage the same sort of poem, albeit in a far more linguistically elaborate manner? Of Thomas as of Tanikawa here, some readers will cry,

'Foul!' They will find for gibberish. This we must not do; instead, we should let the sense hang suspended and allow the emotions to build line by line, cumulatively. Whether a Western reader approves of this phenomenon is altogether another question. It exists. And it exists as a common practice in Japanese poetry.

In poem 33 Tanikawa appears to be earth-bound, though winged and capable of occasional flights to heights not quite blindingly ethereal, for in the last analysis he is engaged in the process rather of assessing the marvels of life and learning to accept them than of contriving mistakenly to flee them or vanquish them. Shall we call him an angel with clipped wings, this creature whom God hath created a little lower than the angels? Poem 41 reads:

> Gazing at the blueness of the sky
> makes me feel I've a place to go back to,
>
> ....
>
> To be is to injure space and time,
> and the pain reproaches me.
> When I'm gone my health will return.

In the divine economy there is no death. There is only that transmogrification that, since he cannot 'be everywhere at once, like light,' finds him finally absent from the earth and present elsewhere —in some corner of eternity from which he initially came and restored to which he will have recovered his perfect essence (as merged with a Timeless, undifferentiated eternity). To exist (to stand out or over against), to be in space and Time, is to exist out of one's element, like a flopping minnow, and hence to be unhealthy and literally in danger of death. Many echoes ricochet off the canyon walls of poem 41, Wordsworth's not the least of these, for once having left his eternal home the poet now flaps around on earth trailing at least some wispy 'clouds of glory.'

In point of fact, however, the poet cannot choose one world over the other and it is that dilemma about which he has made up his mind. A man is in Time but not of it and that is what it means to have clipped wings. There is no escaping this beautiful, lovable jail house of a world, the inmate feeling himself deliciously enriched and blessed by his dilemma. He serves his Time, this lifer, sending his soul on sporadic soirees into the heavens to bring back refreshment as a second breath; nor would he readily have it any other way. The death of Time (this removal back to his origins) would constitute the death of this complex structure of shadowy forms called earth, all of which are to his taste. No, life is not purely edenic, for he at times finds himself now weary now exhilaratingly enlivened now saddened to tears now elated to tears, and faced with these customary swingings of the pendulum he strives, while enduring, to search for an orderliness already innate in the nature of existence. An order from without—a superficial or non-natural order—he does not wish to drag in, establish, and sheepishly obey. He ponders this issue, arguing that life is as it is, an inevitable order of (unreal) Time being a misfortunate aspect of it. There is a wry challenge in one's having to overcome an obstacle that does not exist: Time. The option he chooses is that of looking at Time eye-to-eye, surrendering to it and immersing himself in it—a method not unknown in history. Does the postulant sitting zazen hope to non-think himself out of Time or yet again does he think to absorb Time in such a sponge-like way that Time vanishes? Time flies, when one races ahead of it. The unshot arrow is not subject to Time. Time evaporates when it is subject to benign neglect or when an epiphanal experience lifts one over and out, that itself perhaps constituting a mode of benign neglect.

In these sonnets Tanikawa has not used the word '*tamashii*' that would ordinarily be translated as 'soul.' His word is 'heart,' by which is of course intended the combined powers of 'spirit-feeling-mind'; in a word, 'heart,' as in poem 23:

> Her heart in its transiency
> is hard to measure,
> being too far or too near ....

Heart or soul, however, we do not find engaged in any dueling of the sort philosophy and theology acquaint us with, and which has been amusingly broadcast into fame by Marvell's 'A Dialogue Between the Soul and Body,' where, speaking of its despicable corporeal container, the Soul sarcastically, poignantly pleads, 'O who shall, from this Dungeon, raise/A Soul inslav'd so many wayes?' to which the stung and stinging tongue of

Body replies, 'O who shall me deliver whole/From bonds of this Tyrannic Soul?' I cannot recall anything in Japanese poetic history even faintly similar to Marvell's mode. Soul and Body personified into independent dependencies would simply be unthinkable by Japanese poets, for the world is not perceived as a battlefield on which the forces of good and evil grapple to the death nor is the individual divided within himself into parts that fight one another. The Japanese tendency has rather been for people to accept themselves just as they are, and perhaps even like strands of seaweed afloat on the tide (one ancient poem that I recall in part asks whether then 'like seaweed we [lovers] are destined to float apart, never touching forever'). But isn't Tanikawa actually splitting himself into body and soul? I think not. He doesn't use the word. And the 'heart' which he does use is not meant to be a distinct, discrete entity, as somehow 'soul' is assumed to be in some Western thought.

The sixty-two poems show no serious inclination to research or define eternity in any detail. Having assumed, like Wordsworth, that he came from eternity (true, Wordsworth specifies 'Him'—God— rather than eternity, although whether the former is truly clarifying is doubtful), that that is where he really belongs, and that eventually he will leave the earth and represent himself in and to eternity, he busies himself trying to master the art of living while his Time shall last. It is earth and earthlings that quicken his curiousity. Natural forms are beautiful and they command his attention; however, the sky is empty. Eternity is not peopled; it is not even ensouled. Thus the stars do not twinkle and will not even smile coldly upon you. Eternity is Timeless, undefined, shapeless, amorphic nothingness, a state of non-being better appreciated by the student of Zen than by the astrophysicist. And once out of nature neither he nor Yeats will ever take his shape from those Timely creatures like trees and birds in whose insides an alarm clock has been set ticking towards a deadline.

2 *Nature*:Without nature, nothing, Tanikawa might say. The poems do say so, although his nothing is a nothingness doubtless inferentially superior (preferable) to either something or nothing. Nature itself ('herself' is not an indigenous Japanese idea) is bewilderingly complex and views of nature are, if possible, even more so. Once again, though, we remind ourselves that we are reading poems and that these poems do not delve into nature in any physical, psychological or philosophic detail. Nature merely is

whatever is (except for man-made objects), the customary body of the world comprised of these forms that most commonly appear in *62 Sonnets:* sun-light-wind-sky-birds-people-stars-trees-shadows and, especially, clouds (language is man-made and therefore non-natural; and Tanikawa would probably argue that all nature's forms have existence apart from man's mind). A discussion of creation myths, Homer, Job, Heraclitus, Parmenides, Plato, Aristotle, Virgil, Tasso, Confucius, Chaucer, Milton, Pope, Goethe, Wordsworth, Hegel, Schelling, Einstein, and Suzuki would serve neither the poems' nor our present purposes. Tanikawa consistently and deliberately prefers philosophic simplicity ('transparency,' he calls it in one of the sonnets) and one might here note that however convoluted or avant garde other poetry collections of his sometimes become, they never veer off into distracting philosophic winds. Because his is an instance of it, it *is* possible for a poet to be simultaneously clear and profound, or simple and deep. Such clarity as that at which he sometimes arrives he has purposefully intended and he doggedly maintains it. Openness does not mean naivete any more than ambiguity and vagueness mean confused thinking in Japanese poetry. Tanikawa's words are not the easy mouthings of an armchair philosopher. In my view he has shaped and pruned the garden to an eloquent and disarming lucidity which plays counterpart to shadows, textures, and bends in the path that he walks along. The poetry is one kind of classic Japanese garden, if you will, that creates the hidden (by fences, for example), depth and mystery (by black shadows against white pebbles disappearing between large rocks), ambiguity, ambivalence, contradiction, indecision, and whatnot. And yet one is clear about the controls. They operate effectively, bringing the chaos just up to the point of spillage, and then decisively containing it. The world is not rational. It is a dancing of all forms and shapes, of which man is one, neither the least not the greatest of these. Let contrarieties stand, for honest inconsistency is more interesting than correct, coherent argument (except in mathematics) for the reason that the logic that leads to the closed case also leads to the termination of discussion. Sonnet 21 is instructive:

> When I looked up
> those clouds were gone.
> Not in the amorphous clouds but outside them,
> there's a feeling I'm familiar with.

> Ancient prayers continuously rain down curses
> on those forms.
> When heaven is vacant and earth holds a heart,
> clouds, suspended, aspire to be more than they are.
>
> But what could they become?
> Softly, as though they hope to have hearts,
> they go on annihilating their own shapes.
>
> A full earth
> and a vacant sky
> move me to song.

I do not take this to be an actual personifying of the clouds. Instead the indication is that there is something in the nature of nature such that clouds endlessly change shape, in which sense they 'aspire' to be other than they are. It is a necessity built into the elements and their combinings, in the presence of wind. 'I have a heart. I also am what I am. Clouds do not have a heart. The earth's great beauty, on the one hand, and the sky's emptiness, on the other, move me to writing my poems,' he says.

Still and all, in the next poem he turns around and offers a fairly blatant contradiction of sorts, though one that pretty well falls into place and with which the reader will probably be ready enough to agree (22):

> Real forms have no hearts.
> Forms are transient.
>
> ...
>
> And yet our joy is in trusting in
> and loving forms;
> or rather in trusting in a heart beyond forms.
>
> Today under this too clear sky
> there is only one heart
> and round about us only forms are beautiful.

The clouds 'accepted their own luminosity and then floated away ...' he writes. We are told in 1.2 that the clouds do not have hearts. Are they, possibly, hearts? Time and again Shinto points to certain animate forms and inanimate forms (so-called) and states that these are gods. A specified tree or mountain, for example, is not the abode of a god but itself *is* a god. Is that what clouds are or shall we rather think that clouds are a transitional layer of nature between the temporary fixed forms present on the earth and the formless nothingness the poet calls eternity? Clouds are a class of form conspicuously engaged in changing shape; possessed of a shape in every instant, they are blown in a process of change in which no shape is ever quite repeated. Is Time just a human way of acknowledging shape-changing? Can we conceive of, imagine even, such changes apart from a Time-frame in which they occur? Tanikawa has already claimed, however, that Time does not 'pass' and that there is only the present. Clouds then are just another beautiful form whose nature it is to change visibly, dramatically, and rapidly by contrast with the dull or evidently even idle passage of trees and people.

It is probably true of every basically pre-commercial or trading culture that the world is to be regarded non-exploitatively save at the local level for the sake of communal food, clothing and shelter. Those nomadic groups that farmed the land into infertility did so because they were ignorant of conservation techniques and because they had elsewhere to go; and all the while they worshipped the sun or trees or whatnot, and held selected natural phenomena to be not natural at all but extraordinary and divine. Home was not a galaxy, a planet or a nation. Home was a locale.

This tendency was not untrue of pre-modern Japanese. Clearcutting, strip mining, the massive spewing of industrial poisons into the air or into waterways, and other comprehensive despoilations of the-world-as-home were unknown. (Pre-industrialism means of course that they were not equipped, for one thing, to wreck their environment even if they had been willing to.) To early industrial people and societies 'natural resources' appeared boundless. Further, not just need but greed and genius would impel them to build motorized ships and harpoon guns, and sonar would assist them in endangering several whole species of whales, while affluence and sheer vanity would help them to endanger a species of deer and elephant species for the taking of musk and ivory. Nature on its own account demolished portions of the world's body; demolished portions of its own body as mountains exploded and islands cropped up. For his part, man poisoned and overhunted numerous natural forms into extinction (while, it is fair to say, rescuing others from a threatened extinction not of his making). The air over the cities is rotten and the ozone layer over that is endangered. 'Nor can foot feel, being shod.' Hopkins continued, 'But for all this Nature is never spent./There lives the dearest freshness deep-down things.' At least it was still so in the 19th C. before the profit-takers got deadly serious. No one is exempt. Logging and mining and several industrial processes were as important to you and me in reading Hopkins and Tanikawa as they were to those poets in writing their poems.

This said, the fact still remains that millions of Japanese (say, slightly arbitrarily, those over fifty) do not regard the natural world as a battleground. They may regard the world as a collection of competing and belligerent racial and economic groupings, but—is this paradoxical?—they in some ways respect, or profess respect for, nature. One must not foul one's nest. There still hangs on in Japan (as in every other nation in the world) the ancient taboo against forms of pollution: by death, by blood, for instance. This taboo has held strong against the onslaught of the sciences that teach us that taboos are superstitions and yet the new forms of pollution have not been forestalled or cleaned up, doubtless because we share the nomadic groups' ignorance and in our own right prefer to minimize personal, social, and global ethics. *This* said, nevertheless the Japanese, with Tanikawa made to stand in here as representative, hold the world hospitable and instead of ranting and raving strenuously against the human condition direct their vitriolic discontent these days against big government or big business, whereupon, spleen vented, they return to feeding stray cats, legally protecting barn swallows, shooing hornets out of the house (or using the backdoor so that they can swarm and build around the front), placing plum twigs (made nowadays, ironically, out of oil through dirtying industrial processes) and dandelion blossoms in lunch boxes, and exclaiming over whatever minute or spectacular instances of cuteness or beauty show themselves to the senses. They earn their love of nature through a habitual and close sensory observation. Tanikawa is such an observer, though natural p's and q's are missing from *62 Sonnets.*

He observes it all, not excepting human nature, in figurative ways that can startle without stunning:

> A fast-flying plane flies in the shape of a human passion.
> Though the blue sky pretends to be a backdrop,
> in fact there's nothing there. (30)
>
> Clouds fill up and dispose of themselves; (39)
>
> In a fierce wind
> the earth is like a kite.
>
> ....
>
> Blue sky lies. (45)
>
> But briefly the sun indiscretely illumines everything
> and in that stark naked scenery
> my shadow is blacker than night. (52)

All these utterances are finally referable to human nature, for nature means (intends) nothing save its own best survival conditions. For Tanikawa, as for Wordsworth, observations about natural forms and patterns bespeak something about the character of *human* nature. (Here we might want to look at the contention that while Hopkins was not a 'religious' poet he certainly was a nature poet. I should have thought him, however, a human nature poet.) People invest the world with meaning. There is in people a propensity to create moral structures of such magnitude that even divinities that ought to have created things and structures and to be governing them are imagined and culturally enthroned. Here is a great meaningless world that people have been at pains to make meaningful and beyond which they posit divinity and/or the satanic that operate their respective cities. Of that great world of meaning Time is part and parcel (it is implicit in the *eschaton,* it is implicit in the eternal; it is everywhere).

Tanikawa does not construct a detailed explicit philosophic argument. 'The great beyond' is about as far as he is willing to go ('God' does pop up in several poems) and since his 'eternity' is, *qua* nothingness, indescribable, there is nothing left to say. It is an unfurnished vacuity; the Black Hole of black holes. Can one emotionally comprehend the full sense of a single light-year? The incomparably vaster spatial distances knock insistently on Tanikawa's backdoor all the while that he is professing his love for the real forms of this here-now:

> And my absence is filled with trees, clouds and people.
> My love bears them witness
> and I begin to depend on my absence. (52)

Not just death but 'absence' has left a calling card. He may after all be sharing the same carriage as Emily Dickinson. I take the passage from poem 52 as a way of expressing his consciousness of his own *natural* insignificance; moral judgment not aside (the decision to set moral judgments aside is already a moral judgment), whatever is natural is acceptable and in this premonition of his own death (which means both absence from the earth and non-material presence in some (non)-form otherwise—not to say 'elsewhere'), he sits down to sing in praise of the forms that tarry. By just what line of reasoning he comes to 'accept' his own death other than that the natural is by definition acceptable we are not told. In fairness to the poet we should note that many a man in his thirties and apparently nowhere near to death, and exulting in the secure embrace of good health, has been heard to say that death is a natural event that we should calmly accept. Tanikawa, however, continues, in his mid-sixties, to maintain this position. It was not a young man's bravado. The natural process quietly teaches us that every instance of every form is expandable. Successive instances of them continue to occur, arising and vanishing. Thus it ever naturally has been, and that is good (i.e., natural; 'the way things are': acceptable). And:

> I can possess nothing,
> though I love
> trees, clouds, people. (54)

The determination in these lines is echoed throughout several religious traditions: attachment and non-attachment. However one clings to things, one is always ready to let go; to let go, also, of other people, and of one's very life, which is also said to be not ours to possess. Yet you do not save your life by losing it. Loss of life is an event that inasmuch as it is natural is to be faced and accepted, and, possibly, tentatively welcomed. What does one do and what is to become of one? In 55 he states that:

> Even just sitting around
> I make my life bear fruit,
> not unlike trees that, immobile,
> move in the cosmic circle of life.

In spite of his blindness Milton was not a whit more idle than Tanikawa. Was it is excessive arrogance that drove Milton to claim, 'They also serve who only stand and wait.'? Or by waiting and idling about do both poets actually mean that although their hands are terribly busy all the fuss and bother of writing and operating personal computers doesn't amount to a hill of beans and is just a way of biding their Time until that good (natural) day when they will absent themselves?

Still another idea is introduced in 60 in which Tanikawa writes that while he tries to clarify his feelings to himself, often the world rushes on and leaves him behind. Not only *is* the world richer, he is aware of its being unspeakably richer than he can possibly imagine. A pebble is tossed into a pond and when the tosser looks up from the path of the one expanding ring that his eyes have followed, he finds that other pebbles and other rings and other tossers have entered the picture, and that the world expands beyond his capacity to watch:

> The world moves endlessly, expanding,
> and I can never catch up.
> I continue searching for my heart
> in twilight or in rain or in cirrus clouds.

Among factors that alienate him from the outside world is the relentless grinding of the natural process and the inefficient, imprecise quality of human sensitivity and consciousness. Humans are all dullards and clodpoles. Consider the number of events that take place in and around you in two seconds and the number of those of which you are conscious. We receive and process scant information. This is not a value judgment. It is a fact. Poem 60 also states that:

> Just as wind rustles leaves
> the world ruffles my mind.

only to come back to the final acceptance, in 62:

> I throw myself into
> sky, trees, people,
> that I may soon become part of the world's richness.

This position strikes me as a moving out of self, out of *self*-concern towards an appreciative view of the outside world. The self, split off from eternity, suffers *self*-consciousness and can only mollify its pain by dancing or singing attendance upon the rest of the formal world, thereby becoming at least a bit less self-conscious. The final poem's lines 9-11 make us think that Tanikawa has forgotten what it has been the whole burden of the sonnet sequence to tell us; viz., that he is already 'part of the world's richness' and need not absent himself wholly in order to attain that end. Line 8 is arresting: 'for I am in and of the world.' The second of those prepositions is not entirely persuasive: in the world, yes; but not for long because not of it.

3 *Language*: It is probably accidental that the first of the sonnets in which the poet mentions the writing of his poems is the only one of the sixty-two in which relative depression and disconcertion gather into a cloud that casts a broad shadow over the poem. Here is 9 in its entirety:

> Society is nothing but
> a human logjam;
> and loneliness nothing but
> one miserable specimen.
>
> Bewilderment.
> I'm completely bewildered.
> God uses me
> and politicians try to, too.

> All kinds of things—girls, catching cold, philosophy—
> all these bewilder me.
> Fate wants to work in detail.
>
> *And so this line of verse as a diversion.* [italics mine]
> No one cares what I say:
> Will that make some fool think I'm a loner?

Nowhere else in *62 Sonnets* can I find this sentiment so strongly stated. Does he say elsewhere that depression and perplexity are his motives for writing? I cannot find where poem 9 simply catches him in an off-moment; he appears (line 13) even maudlin. As a matter of fact the radical isolation that a poet sometimes feels as a result of his being 'misunderstood' or ignored or as a result of other forms of hurt that he thinks he suffers at the hands of other people will serve him only to a limited degree as a cause of poems. Tanikawa is a highly social creature, a confident, open, humble, convivial communicator, and this needs to be remarked so that poem 9 can be seen in clarifying context. It should be stated that his poems arise out of a joy of life and out of fellow-feeling, and not out of the psychology of the victim.

At the same time one should remark the frequent occasions in his collected poetry—at times also evident in this book—when he is not in the mood or of a mind to write a poem. (In *62 Sonnets* he uses the word for 'song,' which can mean one kind of poem, instead of the existing word for 'poem,' perhaps because the Italian 'sonnetto'—little song—happily coincides with the word ('*uta*') that Tanikawa uses.) His little sounds or songs were certainly not meant for singing nor in any case is that what was originally intended by the word 'lyric.' Lyric was merely one of three general branches of poetry as distinct from narrative and dramatic. Tanikawa's poems resemble little songs—and many Western sonnets—in that their heightened emotional pitch urges them towards music. A certain plainness of address and familiarity of tone joined to an occasional off-handed narrative element looking something like conversation, on the one hand, or talking to oneself, on the other, finally militate against the poems' wanting to be sung. That and the overall stanzaic pattern, uninterrupted throughout, justify the title choice. Each of the sixty-two is of fourteen lines divided into stanzas of 4-4-3 and 3 lines, respectively. Rhyme and meter in Western senses are not present nor does any classic tool of Japanese prosody operate. The poems are of course characterized by his personal speech and syntactical rhythms and he eschews rhetoric and other literary devices and opts for simple words and diction. Looking back at the uses and the milieu of such poets as Masaika Shiki, Miyazawa Kenji, and Hagiwara Sakutaro, and then having for the first time read Tanikawa's volume, *Tabi*, one of my colleagues blurted out, apropos of Tanikawa's work, 'But where's the poetry!') Often, as in poem 14, Tanikawa just doesn't wish to sing at all:

> Without a song, without will,
>
> . . . .
>
> People sing amiss.
> They have no words to utter nothingness
> and no words to utter anything.
>
> But where I'm standing there is everything:
> people on the street, grass in the field, and,
> in the heavens, nothingness.

Pretty early on in the sequence then we have met up with an idea commonly reiterated in Tanikawa's work that words are inadequate. In one of his later collections *(Coca-Cola Lessons)* a street drunk proclaims in thrashing, guttural slurs that there is 'real poetry' in his thrashing, guttural slurs ('Aahhh-wahhhh!'), whereas the poet's words 'is nuthin but printed words,' and he dares the poet to try to get the true poetry of his drunken nonsense down on paper. In poem 23, here and here alone calling his songs by another name, he identifies the problematic character of poems. Made of language, they yet arise out of the non-verbal, albeit overflowing, heart and as such should really be directed to the speechless emotions (namely, to the heart): ' ... this morning my letter is not addressed to the mind.' Words, words, words—the Japanese universally contend that if *kotoba* (words) is what the Chinese have a penchant for then *kokoro* (mind-spirit-heart) is the genius of the Japanese. The very word is ubiquitous at all levels, in all endeavors of Japanese life (curiously, even *kokoro* is a word, however) and one of their most celebrated novels is called not *kotoba* but *Kokoro* (Soseki's).

Just because of the torturous connection that joins 'kokoro' to 'kotoba'. Tanikawa is veritably obsessed with the word 'kotoba' and is as frustrated by the necessity to use words as he is desirous of dispensing with them altogether and letting *kokoro* reign supreme. However silent he may wish to remain, he fidgets and worries words into poems whose 'message' is that he has nothing to say. The heart is full but what fills the heart is inexpressible and poems that hazard to express the heart can but palely and distortingly do their job of translation. Emotional plenitude is its own reward and expressiveness. Koan: when is a poem not a poem? There are Western ways to cope with such dilemmas: 'That's nothing but a cop-out' or 'Well, let's talk about it' or 'That certainly sounds childish,' *et cetera*. *Kokoro* and *kotoba* are not at odds; they simply emerge from different premises and occupy different spheres of discourse, until, that is, the effort is made to translate the one (*kokoro*) in terms, literally, of the other (*kotoba*). Now the battle is joined. Poem 30:

> I won't let words rest.
> At times they feel ashamed of themselves
> and want to die inside of me.
>
> ....
>
> When I call out, in a small voice,
> the world doesn't answer.
> My words are no different from those of the birds.

'I shout ... I keep on singing.' (31) And then, in moving from the turmoil of poem 31 to poem 38:

> There's a midnight exchange
> of tiny whispered words.
> The songs of day are frozen
> and over them whispers keep on sliding.

> The shapes of life are sharpened
> in the silence
> after the shrill cry of sinister birds.
>
> I'm the story-teller.
> After the wind has borne my ineloquence away
> from the distance 'Love...' comes back.

In some other volumes Tanikawa joins battle immediately. The delay in doing so in *62 Sonnets* results from his uncertainty about the problem that life-*cum*-language generates, especially for the poet. What does language have to do with primary experience (apart from or prior to language usage)? What can language do with reality? One answer is that it does nothing. Then the question comes, isn't poetry (as *kotoba*) an impediment in our quest to assess the direct encounter with reality called experience? Tanikawa answers in the affirmative. Yet in so answering he has written himself into a sticky corner: he is a poet; he uses words; *and* he has nothing to say except that words get in the way and he wishes to goodness they would get out of the way and let him (and his immediate experience) be. No wonder he often feels decidedly like *not* writing poems. At this point we understand him to be, like Hopkins, like Wordsworth, no nature-poet whatsoever except as a human nature poet, forgetful of the assertive sky and insistent upon asserting himself. He is in good company—the traditional company of humane literati who assert themselves poetically. Even silent, silenced, he is bound to take pencil in hand and say so. What effect he has on the world and how efficacious he deems himself are different questions. Poem 50's question gives way to insightful self-awareness:

> Don't things complain in their anxiety
> about just being called
> a cup, a tree,
> a daughter, a picture ...?

> I know that things certainly do exist,
> but can you name anything
> apart from people?
>
> It's fairly easy for nothing to exist.
> Call as I will, the world doesn't waken.
> All I can do is love foolishly.

Indeed the futility of language and the uselessness of the poet, as self-perceived, now and again reduce him to the level of Tennyson's 'child crying in the night' on this 'puny star' of a world which is 'in the middle of nowhere.' Poem 56 states that:

> In such moments
> I collect the little names of things
> and somehow
> I lapse into silence.

The world's other voices make more sense and sound out to greater effect than does language:

> Now and then sounds call to the world,
> more confidently than my song:
> distant whistles, barking, the paper-boy ....
>
> In such moments the world is listening,
> as breathlessly as twilight,
> reaffirming itself sound by sound.

This mood continues through poem 57:

> In the song I sing
> the world is wounded.
> I try to make it sing
> but it stays silent.

> Words are poor little kids
> forever lost
> who perch on things, like dragonflies trembling
> in the midst of dense silence.
>
> ....
>
> They curse me and die,
> snatched up by a star-bright sky.
> I sell their corpses.

Words are cicada husks, the genuine article having sloughed off its shell and fled. Frail, feckless, homeless, they flutter in dark immensity and are swallowed up. The ashamed poet admits to exploiting these linguistic gnats and actually selling them to readers. Non-verbal sound is an improvement on poetry. And before he can get around to singing his song nature has beat him to it:

> Falling rain ...
> a girl running ...
> and oh—the wind:
> these are already my song. (59)

His song is tossed up and out into the air. Who, he asks in 61, will listen? As they fall back to earth he finds:

> It's better for joy to return to earth,
> for then joy doesn't die in solitude.
>
> You don't need to confess
> love.
> The world will see it in your eyes.

Language and the employment of it suggest to Tanikawa that a reality lies beyond words, first of all on this earth but then also out of this world. For the grasping of that fact words are required and yet they themselves are irrelevant to that fact. They are a screen through which reality is filtered, bruised and maimed as it is in the process. Tanikawa's own language is sometimes vague, general, imprecise or abstract, such that the reality which he thinks irrefragable behind the words cannot push itself clearly into consciousness. Ultimate reality ought to be unclear and so should language which is used to point to it. It is appropriate that strictly speaking Tanikawa's language is now and again unclear, and that in treating the matter of 'eternity' it is uniformly unclear.

For Tanikawa life is unclear, too—not just reality. The search for reality beneath natural forms is largely unsuccessful because its properties (if it has any) are not susceptible of rational (or linguistic) clarification and, besides, reality evidently has no need to be other than what it is. The need is man's. The need is the poet's need to speak. The poems leave reality as they find it: it exists apart from human language and does not come when called. And the poems' complexity and honest imprecision merely mirror their subject.

4a *Knowledge (a posteriori)*: Tanikawa, not unnaturally, gives scant evidence for his acceptance of knowledge as a product of direct observation or experimentation. It is just a premise adopted from the outset that goes unargued. There are facts, he would say, common-sensically available and open to anyone's observation. Can the world be a material phantasm? Materiality is real but it is not ultimate. In poem 21 he observes:

> When I looked up
> those clouds were gone.

and in 29:

> ...
> The winter sunlight that warms my fingers
> also falls across today's empty chair.
>
> Between the window's outside and inside
> a fragment of the world is suspended.
> As I reach to touch it
> the beautiful thing gallops away.

This observation on reflection at first blush strikes a mysterious note to the reflective poet and reader, even though reflection is a natural phenomenon and the four lines are readable, surely, in a sense acceptable to humane physicists. The reflection is in the window. A patch of garden, say, holding rocks and selected branches hangs in the windowpane until in moving to touch it he changes the angle of vision and the reflection vanishes. *Does* it vanish? Is there a reflection in that glass when there is no one there to see it? Where does it go? Can a reflection be touched? Physics and physiology indeed present some hard mysteries; some of the lovely ones give us pause.

Nevertheless we are talking essentially about human nature which, in thoughtful observation, will directly lead us to sanity about this earthly enterprise and our place in it. Poem 39 reads:

> When people realize they are part of an extension
> they start talking tough; e.g.,
> 'I'm more important than trees.'
>
> Thus, inaudibly, the trees whisper,
> 'It's important, not to sing
> but to empty your hearts.'

By their being, we understand, a silent and vital carrier of and donor to the life-process, the trees 'say' something moral to the poet. The voiceless trees have spoken for him; we must speak up for one another.

The matter of physical reflection enters the sequence for the second time in poem 48. Life, Tanikawa believes, is only a walking shadow—real enough, since it does exist yet its existence is comparable to that of a reflection: brief and fragmented, it is not its own cause or creator. The poem moves easily in and out of empirical data and speculation:

> We often hear the dark side of life
> referred to solemnly:
> graves, hearses, wills ....
> These tell us nothing about death.

> The living cannot see beyond shadows
> and don't know what it's like to lose nothing.
> Surrounded by mirrors,
> we're always peeping into life in reflection.
>
> Since death lacks mirrors
> we shall soon be unselfconscious
> and able to be one with the world ....
>
> But in the rainy street today the living are busy living.
> The evening paper reports suicides:
> we're nothing but the distance that surrounds death.

(In, that is, the columns of a newspaper.) Since ultimate reality is an indivisible blankness, death, which is also that, reclaims us for eternity. Yet three poems later (51) he claims that:

> The single-mindedness of things foredoomed tempts me
> towards simple thoughts;
> only, in this familiar moment
> death will not inhibit my thoughts.
>
> Under the silence of sky and sun
> this moment is constantly being snatched away,
> and the pain of it scares me.
>
> But I return into the world.
> No day is without its partings, is it?
> To that world I return.

An embracing of the world is called for and together with a curiosity about eternity an embracing of that world, as well. His dreams are no more of an escapist variety than his speculations are demented, and he is sufficiently the realist to have seen that, beyond a point, speculation leads nowhere, least of all to the eternity he projects, because the unknown will not yield to rational or fanciful speculation, much less to logic. Will dreams unveil eternity for us? We do not know; cannot be sure; and the unknown must remain the unknown just because we have no way of getting there before our Time. If we cannot cling to eternity we *can* cling to the world, believing in it and believing moreover that when Time comes to let go we go to a far, far better place—we have been there before—than the world of here-now in Time. That bit of knowledge is not *a posteriori*.

4b *Knowledge (a priori)*: Hunches, insights, intuitions (as in direct apprehensions of morality)—this category of knowledge arrived at independently of observation or testing has its place in *62 Sonnets*. Whether the posture is that of faith that such-and-such is the case is inconsequential. Tanikawa's *a priori* knowledge, further, is at least as visionary as propositional. The 'eternity' he envisions is given the form of that word and the conditions of Timelessness, placelessness, and unknowableness. It portends nothing(ness). There is a long argument whose conclusion is that *a priori* knowledge is not open to argument. On the matter of heaven, eternity, nothing-ness, and other names severally given to 'states' that refer to non-life or non-earthly life or the after-life and the like, Tanikawa is in good company, surrounded by a great crowd of witnesses. If his certainty about eternity proves wrong (how can knowledge prove wrong?) he will be found wrong along with hundreds of millions of believers across many centuries representing numerous religious and philosophic communities. Poem 7 reads:

> Death comes out of the earth,
> out of the future.
> ....

If he does not mean that young forms like minnows, saplings, sprouts, and babies are growing toward their eventual absence, then the statement is in the nature of the *a priori* and is not on the face of it self-explanatory:

> But the heart must go on, responsive to everything,
> always starting to live anew, beginning here
> and negotiating the distances.

This would have the character of a moral truth apprehended directly, though psychologically explicable, for example, with respect to our everyday lives; to wit, that for health's sake we ought to keep growing, getting to know ourselves and one another better and better, and eliminating an inch at a Time the disabling gaps in our knowledge. On the other hand there is that about the 'heart ... expanding' and 'negotiating the distances' that tries to point us toward the stars and toward eternity. Is he speaking of the human connection to eternity? So it seems to me. Perhaps like Vaughan he 'saw Eternity the other night.' The envisaging is given an earthier turn in poem 10:

> Wind blew over the earth and an unknown star.
> God walked on the earth at evening,
> and also on an unknown star.

What in the world is going on in these lines? Has he been reading *Genesis* or Blake's *Jerusalem,* or *Paradise Lost,* or looking at Burne Jones's paintings? The cosmography indicates that all planetary bodies are interconnected, linked by wind and the agency of 'God.' It is more than Tennyson's ' ... whole round Earth ... ' that ' ... is every way/Bound by gold chains about the feet of God.' It is the whole of existence. Origin and destination matter to him, though decidedly absent is any interest in an ethical platform or a theological credo imposed by historical religious communities and their institutions. Theology bores him. He will settle for God and eternity, as far as destination is concerned. The ethic he will live by will be one sensitively and painfully wrought out of his daily experience, including the daily experience of writing (or not writing) poems.

I should describe Tanikawa's pilgrimage as being fraught with deep and painful struggle, except that to look at his poems cursorily you would never know it. There is no chest-thumping, gnashing of teeth, or any other kind of public display of agony. He is not just passive, either. His is the way of quiet, patient and—let us say it— healthy handling of his sometimes troubled and hurtful life. He wears no hair shirt. And he is normally much too delighted with the world's forms to waste Time on poisoned emotions.

A priori knowledge? Look at poem 13:

> In a song that is ever silent
> signs of God are faintly felt
>
> ....
> Passion can fill anything
> under the silently shining sun and sky,
> which are overflowing.

By now, however, we recollect contrarieties. The heavens are empty yet full. Eternity is nothingness yet God strolls the stars. But consistency is the hobgoblin of insecure minds and mathematicians, and is more important in the making of cement and pasta than in the making of some poems that move us. Visions are not logical arguments:

> The heavens are forever a tedious stage setting.
> Since everything is under them,
> they become the measuring rod of distance. (36)

The sky is a source of endless knowledge. In one sonnet 'The sky is a benevolent lie.' In another it is not a canopy but a well into which he flings himself in order to find himself. And in 36 we measure distance by the sky, among the possible meanings of which is that by the sky's very vastness and ubiquity we come to know the human place in the scheme of things as well as how many removes we are from a highly unplatonic eternal ideal.

We come in poem 49 to a person who appears as a giver and taker in the poet's love life. His 'love' is said elsewhere to have nowhere to go, 'like nostalgia'; however, as he gives love to the world so is he able to receive it. It is most blessed to give and to receive:

> ....
> Let me nurture desire in all its tenderness
> so as to snatch love back from the world.

> I look at her
> and life's shapes bring me back to the world.
> A young tree and her figure
> sometimes meet in me.
> What I learn in touching her closed lips,
> without naming my feelings,
> is carried away by a vast silence.
>
> Yet in that moment I am also that silence.
> Like a tree, I, too,
> snatch love from the world.

All natural forms (man also) constitute the world in the way that fungus and alga constitute lichen: symbiotically. The chlorophyll in this metaphysical photosynthetic process is love. The final poem's full sense is not altogether instantly clear, to me anyway, but I take it to suggest something like this: 'My sense of my own alienation from the world or from much of the world and from other people is made tolerable by the experience of human love. In calling to the woman I love and who loves me, I suddenly feel the wonderful and weighty presence of the earth and my modest but actual place in it. As that knowledge dawns upon me my self-importance dies away (and at the same time I somehow feel the sense in which I am in and of eternity).'

EPILOGUE

Tanikawa invariably states that poems are afterthoughts; after, that is, the experiences which are their subjects, and no happy substitute at that. By his admission (in an interview published in a January 1987 number of Tokyo's *The Student Times*) he is primarily concerned about something besides poems, in the ordinary experience of life (exclusive of the literary experience that for him is also ordinary). What offhand sounds shocking is that a professional poet is less interested in poems than in living. It is not shocking, really. Nearly all human activity reflects areas of experience larger and more momentous than activity *per se*. Chisel and stethoscope serve ends beyond the immediate. So do poems. In multiple matters of the heart (medical or psychological), a statement of Schopenhauer's comes back to me from the time I encountered it—in *The World as Will and Idea*,—back in the early 1950's. I am ashamed not to recall the translator's name but I have his translation, apparently for life: 'Man has an instinct for rhythmic patterns which embraces an entire world of forms.' Aristotle had said something similar. But Schopenhauer's expression fits Tanikawa to a T. Speech and silence, prefix and suffix, preface and postfix, prelude and coda, warp and woof, epithalamium and elegy, turn and return are some of the terms that indicate the cyclical character of life, or anyway our apparent desire for such. Balance and conclusiveness are thought necessary and hence satisfying in just about every human activity, in our diets as in our bowling alleys, in commerce as in dance. Lacking these rhythmic patterns which we instinctively desire, look for, and create, short and long distances cannot be negotiated. Patterns such Tanikawa's *62 Sonnets* build us a bridge over distance at once serviceable and beautiful.

W.I.E

This double volume presents the sixth and seventh books of Mr. Tanikawa to be translated by William I. Elliott and Kawamura Kazuo. The other five are —

from Prescott Street Press, Portland, Oregon: *With Silence My Companion*, 1975; *At Midnight in the Kitchen I Just Wanted to Talk to You*, 1980; *Coca Cola Lessons*, 1986;

from Prescott Street Press, Portland, Oregon, and Shichosha, Tokyo: *Floating the River in Melancholy* (bilingual), 1988 — winner of the 1989 American Book Award;

from Seidosha, Tokyo: *Songs of Nonsense* (bilingual), 1991.

LIBRARY